Introduction

- Introducing the power of Corel Draw in professional design.

- Why mastering Corel Draw is essential for professionals.

Chapter 1: Navigating the Corel Draw Interface Like a Pro

- Exploring the interface: tools, panels, and workspace customization.

- Keyboard shortcuts for efficient workflow.

- Utilizing workspaces and layouts for various design   needs.

Chapter 2: Mastering Vector Illustration Techniques

- Advanced shape manipulation using node editing.

- Creating complex vector artwork with the Bézier tool.

- Working with layers and object management for   organized   designs.

Chapter 3: Harnessing the Power of Typography

- Fine-tuning text using advanced formatting options.

- Creating custom text effects and artistic typography.

- Handling text along paths and within shapes.

Chapter 4: Beyond the Basics: Advanced Drawing and Design Techniques

- Exploring gradient mesh for realistic shading and highlights.

- Blend tool techniques for smooth transitions and creative effects.

- Creating intricate patterns using the Pattern Fill tool.

Chapter 5: Masterful Photo Editing and Manipulation

- Understanding photo effects: retouching, enhancing, and creative edits.

- Working with masks and clipping paths for precise image control.

- Combining vector and raster elements seamlessly.

Chapter 6: Dynamic Artwork with Blends, Brushes, and Effects

- Utilizing blends and contours for dynamic shapes and gradients.

- Designing custom brushes for unique artistic effects.

- Applying and customizing special effects for eye-catching designs.

Chapter 7: Professional Print and Digital Output

- Preparing designs for print: CMYK, DPI, and color management.

- Exporting for web and digital media with optimal settings.

- Tips for collaborating with printers and other professionals.

Chapter 8: Time-Saving Techniques for Efficient Workflows

- Creating templates and styles for consistent design aesthetics.

- Using libraries and symbols for reusable design elements.

- Automating tasks with scripts and macros.

Chapter 9: Advanced Tips for Illustration and Logo Design

- Designing intricate logos using vector tools and techniques.

- Combining shapes and effects for professional logo creation.

- Strategies for simplifying complex ideas into memorable logos.

Chapter 10: Pushing the Boundaries: 3D Design and Perspective

- Exploring Corel Draw's 3D tools and capabilities.

- Designing 3D objects with depth, shading, and perspective.

- Integrating 3D elements into 2D designs seamlessly.

Chapter 11: Creative Tips for UI/UX Design and Web Graphics

- Designing user interfaces with precision and aesthetics.

- Optimizing web graphics for fast loading and responsiveness.

- Creating interactive elements and prototypes within Corel Draw.

Conclusion
- Reflecting on the journey from novice to professional in Corel Draw.

- Emphasizing the importance of continuous learning and experimentation.

- Encouraging readers to apply the tips and tricks to their own design projects.

Appendix: Keyboard Shortcuts and Quick References
- A handy reference guide to essential keyboard shortcuts.

- Quick tips and references for frequently used tools and functions.

Glossary
- Definitions of key terms and concepts used throughout the ebook.

Introduction

INTRODUCING THE POWER OF COREL DRAW IN PROFESSIONAL DESIGN

In the realm of graphic design, where creativity meets functionality, having a versatile and powerful design tool at your disposal is essential. Corel Draw, a longstanding contender in the graphic design software arena, has established itself as a go-to platform for both beginners and seasoned professionals. Its intuitive interface, rich feature set, and flexibility make it a standout choice for various design projects. In this article, we'll delve into the power of Corel Draw in professional design and explore how it has become an indispensable tool for designers around the world.

A Comprehensive Design Ecosystem

Corel Draw isn't just a software; it's a comprehensive design ecosystem that empowers designers to bring their creative visions to life. Whether you're an illustrator, logo designer, typographer, or even a UI/UX designer, Corel Draw offers a range of tools and features tailored to your needs. From vector illustration and typography to photo editing and layout design, Corel Draw provides an all-in-one solution that eliminates the need for switching between multiple software applications.

Intuitive Interface and User-Friendly Experience

One of the most appealing aspects of Corel Draw is its intuitive interface. For professionals who value efficiency and seamless workflows, Corel Draw's user-friendly experience is a game-changer. The interface is thoughtfully organized, with tools and panels logically arranged for easy access. Whether you're a newcomer or a seasoned designer, you can quickly become familiar with the software's layout, saving you valuable time that can be channeled into the creative process itself.

Unleashing Creativity with Advanced Features

While Corel Draw's accessibility is impressive, its true power lies in its advanced features that cater to professionals seeking to push their creative boundaries. For vector illustration, the node editing capabilities provide unparalleled control over shapes and curves. This allows designers to create intricate and complex designs with precision.

Typography enthusiasts will appreciate Corel Draw's typography tools that enable fine-tuning of text, artistic text effects, and seamless integration of text within shapes and paths. This attention to detail is what distinguishes professional designs from the ordinary.

Blending Art and Technology

Corel Draw bridges the gap between traditional artistry and modern technology. The software's blend tool, for instance, offers the capability to create smooth transitions between shapes, making it an invaluable asset for artists seeking to infuse their designs with dynamic movement. Moreover, the inclusion of 3D design and perspective features adds a new dimension (literally) to the creative process, allowing designers to craft three-dimensional elements within their two-dimensional designs.

Efficiency and Consistency in Professional Workflows

In the fast-paced world of professional design, time is of the essence. Corel Draw recognizes this need and equips designers with tools to enhance their efficiency. Customizable workspaces, keyboard shortcuts, and the ability to create and save design templates expedite the design process, ensuring that projects are completed on time without compromising quality.

Furthermore, Corel Draw's consistency-enhancing features, such as libraries and symbols, enable designers to maintain uniformity across various projects. This is particularly beneficial for branding and corporate identity design, where consistency is key.

Conclusion

In the realm of professional design, Corel Draw stands as a powerhouse of creative tools and features that cater to designers' diverse needs. From vector illustration to typography, photo editing to 3D design, Corel Draw provides a holistic solution that fosters both artistry and efficiency. Its intuitive interface, advanced capabilities, and emphasis on optimizing workflows make it an indispensable tool for designers who are passionate about their craft and are committed to delivering top-notch design work.

Whether you're a seasoned professional looking to take your designs to the next level or an aspiring designer eager to explore the realm of graphic design, Corel Draw's power and versatility will undoubtedly be your ally on your creative journey.

WHY MASTERING COREL DRAW IS ESSENTIAL FOR PROFESSIONALS

In the ever-evolving landscape of graphic design, staying ahead of the curve is crucial for professionals seeking to create impactful and memorable visual experiences. Among the arsenal of design tools available, Corel Draw emerges as a cornerstone for professionals looking to elevate their craft. In this comprehensive article, we'll delve into the reasons why mastering Corel Draw is not just beneficial, but essential for professionals in the creative industry.

Versatility Unleashed

At the heart of Corel Draw's appeal is its versatility. Professionals in various design disciplines, from illustration to typography, packaging design to web graphics, can harness its array of tools and features to accomplish their creative goals. The software's ability to accommodate a diverse range of projects under one roof makes it a cost-effective and efficient choice for professionals who wear many design hats.

Seamless Interface for Streamlined Workflows

In the world of professional design, time is a precious resource. Corel Draw understands this implicitly and offers an intuitive interface that streamlines workflows. From the moment you open the software, you're greeted with a well-organized workspace that allows easy access to essential tools and panels. Professionals can quickly navigate through projects, experiment with design variations, and make real-time adjustments, ensuring that the creative process remains uninterrupted and productive.

Precision and Control in Design

Mastering Corel Draw equips professionals with the ability to exercise precision and control over their designs. The software's vector-based approach ensures that designs remain crisp and scalable, whether they're destined for business cards or billboards. With node editing capabilities, designers can manipulate shapes and curves to create intricate and complex designs that stand out in a crowded visual landscape.

Typography that Speaks Volumes

In the realm of design, typography is more than just text; it's a visual expression of communication. Corel Draw recognizes this and offers a robust set of typography tools. Professionals can explore a wide range of font options, fine-tune text formatting, and even create custom text effects that add personality and flair to their designs. The software's ability to integrate text seamlessly within shapes and along paths opens up a world of creative possibilities for typographic artistry.

From Concept to Reality: Advanced Design Techniques

One of the hallmarks of a professional designer is the ability to transform ideas into tangible visual experiences. Corel Draw empowers professionals to do just that through its advanced design techniques. The blend tool, for instance, allows designers to create smooth transitions and dynamic effects between shapes, adding a touch of sophistication to their work. Whether it's intricate vector illustrations, realistic photo editing, or 3D design, Corel Draw equips professionals with the tools to bring their creative visions to life.

Enhancing Collaboration and Communication

In the professional design sphere, effective collaboration and communication are non-negotiable. Corel Draw recognizes this and offers features that facilitate both. The software's compatibility with other industry-standard formats ensures that designs can be seamlessly shared and edited across different platforms. Whether you're collaborating with team members or presenting your designs to clients, Corel Draw's export options and print-ready features simplify the process, ensuring that your work is showcased in the best possible light.

A Lifelong Learning Journey

Mastering Corel Draw isn't just a destination; it's a journey of continuous learning and growth. As the software evolves, so do the possibilities it offers. Professional designers who invest time in mastering Corel Draw position themselves to adapt to new design trends and techniques. The software's robust community and access to online resources further enhance the learning experience, creating a supportive environment for professionals to expand their skill set.

Conclusion

In the dynamic and competitive realm of professional design, mastering Corel Draw isn't just an option; it's a strategic decision. The software's versatility, user-friendly interface, precision tools, and advanced design capabilities make it an indispensable asset for professionals who strive for excellence. From typography that communicates emotion to vector illustrations that captivate audiences, Corel Draw empowers designers to create with impact and purpose. By embracing Corel Draw, professionals embark on a journey that not only enhances their design prowess but also enables them to shape the visual narratives of tomorrow.

Chapter 1: Navigating the Corel Draw Interface Like a Pro

EXPLORING THE INTERFACE: TOOLS, PANELS, AND WORKSPACE CUSTOMIZATION

In the world of graphic design, a designer's creative journey begins with the interface of their chosen design software. Corel Draw, a powerhouse in the design realm, offers an interface that is both intuitive and customizable, catering to the diverse needs of professionals and creatives alike. In this in-depth article, we will dive into the intricacies of exploring the Corel Draw interface, including its tools, panels, and the invaluable ability to customize your workspace.

Navigating the Toolset: A Creative Toolkit at Your Fingertips

At the core of the Corel Draw interface lies a comprehensive set of tools that empower designers to create with precision and finesse. From the Pen tool, which allows for intricate vector illustration, to the Shape tool for creating geometric designs, each tool serves as a brushstroke on the canvas of creativity. The user-friendly layout ensures that these tools are easily accessible, while their functionalities can be quickly grasped by both newcomers and seasoned professionals.

Harnessing the Power of Panels

Adjacent to the tools, the panels in Corel Draw play a pivotal role in enhancing efficiency and optimizing workflows. The Layers panel, for instance, allows designers to organize elements of their designs with ease, facilitating quick adjustments and edits. The Color and Swatches panels simplify the process of selecting and applying colors, while the Object Manager provides a hierarchical view of design components, ensuring that no detail goes unnoticed.

Workspace Customization: Tailoring the Interface to Your Needs

One of the standout features of Corel Draw is its flexibility in allowing designers to customize their workspace. No two designers work in the exact same way, and Corel Draw recognizes this by offering a range of customization options. Designers can arrange panels to suit their preferences, create personalized toolsets for frequently used functions, and even define their own keyboard shortcuts for streamlined workflows.

Creating Multiple Workspaces: A Palette of Possibilities

Corel Draw takes workspace customization a step further by enabling the creation of multiple workspaces. This feature is particularly valuable for professionals who engage in diverse design projects.

With a few clicks, a designer can transition from an illustration-centric workspace to one optimized for typography, adjusting the arrangement of tools and panels to align with the task at hand. This dynamic approach ensures that the interface adapts to the designer's creative rhythm.

Aesthetic and Functional Harmony

Workspace customization isn't just about personal preference; it's about achieving a harmonious blend of aesthetics and functionality. Designers can choose from a variety of pre-designed workspaces tailored to specific design tasks, ensuring that the tools and panels required for that task are easily accessible. This approach not only enhances efficiency but also minimizes distractions, allowing designers to focus solely on the creative process.

Enhancing Collaboration and Sharing

In a collaborative design environment, the ability to share workspace layouts becomes invaluable. Corel Draw recognizes this need and allows designers to export and import their customized workspaces. Whether you're working within a team or transitioning between devices, the ability to replicate your preferred workspace ensures consistency in design approach and enhances collaboration.

Conclusion

Exploring the Corel Draw interface is akin to embarking on a journey of creative discovery. The carefully designed tools, panels, and workspace customization options empower designers to navigate seamlessly between imagination and creation. From the intricacies of vector manipulation to the finesse of typography, Corel Draw's interface serves as a bridge between a designer's vision and the tangible design outcomes. As professionals and creatives continue to push the boundaries of design, Corel Draw's interface evolves alongside them, adapting to the ever-changing landscape of creativity.

KEYBOARD SHORTCUTS FOR EFFICIENT WORKFLOW

In the fast-paced world of graphic design, time is a precious commodity. Designers are constantly seeking ways to streamline their workflows and increase productivity without compromising the quality of their work. One powerful technique that often gets overlooked is the strategic use of keyboard shortcuts. In this in-depth article, we will delve into the world of keyboard shortcuts and explore how they can significantly enhance your efficiency and creativity within Corel Draw.

The Power of Keyboard Shortcuts

Keyboard shortcuts are like secret pathways that unlock hidden treasures within a software application. Corel Draw is no exception, offering a plethora of keyboard shortcuts that allow designers to perform tasks quickly and seamlessly. These shortcuts eliminate the need to navigate through menus and panels, providing a direct route to the tools and functions you need.

Navigating the Interface with Ease

From selecting tools to executing complex commands, keyboard shortcuts offer a swift and fluid way to navigate the Corel Draw interface. Need to switch to the Selection tool? Simply press "V." Want to access the Text tool? Press "T." Memorizing these shortcuts transforms your keyboard into a control center, reducing the time spent on repetitive actions.

Boosting Efficiency with Modifier Keys

Corel Draw takes keyboard shortcuts to the next level by incorporating modifier keys. By combining the Ctrl, Alt, and Shift keys with specific letters or numbers, you can execute a multitude of tasks. For instance, Ctrl + C copies selected objects, while Ctrl + V pastes them. Shift + X swaps the fill and outline colors, and Alt + Ctrl + Z undoes multiple actions in sequence. The judicious use of modifier keys further enhances your efficiency, allowing you to accomplish complex actions effortlessly.

Personalization for Optimal Productivity

What makes keyboard shortcuts even more powerful is the ability to personalize them. Corel Draw allows you to customize existing shortcuts or assign your own to specific functions. This feature is particularly valuable if you find yourself frequently using certain tools or commands. By aligning shortcuts with your workflow and preferences, you create a tailor-made experience that maximizes productivity.

Shortcut Combinations for Advanced Functions

As you delve deeper into Corel Draw, you'll discover that many tasks have multi-step processes. Keyboard shortcuts can be your allies in navigating these intricacies. For instance, Ctrl + Shift + K brings up the Convert to Curves dialog box, enabling you to transform text into editable vector curves. Ctrl + Shift + C combines selected objects, and Ctrl + Shift + G ungroups them. These multi-key shortcuts grant you quick access to advanced functions, allowing you to execute complex tasks effortlessly.

The Learning Curve and Mastery

Mastering keyboard shortcuts does involve a learning curve, especially if you're new to Corel Draw or graphic design software in general. However, the investment in time and effort is well worth it. Like learning a musical instrument, it's a gradual process that yields increasing proficiency over time. As your muscle memory develops, you'll find yourself naturally reaching for shortcuts without conscious thought, enabling you to focus more on the creative process itself.

Conclusion

In the dynamic world of graphic design, every second counts. Keyboard shortcuts offer a valuable solution to the perpetual challenge of optimizing workflow efficiency. By incorporating these shortcuts into your design routine, you not only save time but also cultivate a more intuitive and seamless creative experience. Whether you're a novice or a seasoned professional, the journey of mastering keyboard shortcuts in Corel Draw is a journey toward increased productivity, enhanced creativity, and a more refined approach to your design endeavors.

UTILIZING WORKSPACES AND LAYOUTS FOR VARIOUS DESIGN NEEDS

In the realm of graphic design, adaptability is key. Designers constantly switch between different projects, each with its unique set of tools, panels, and requirements. Corel Draw, a versatile design software, recognizes this need for flexibility and offers a powerful feature set that includes customizable workspaces and layouts. In this comprehensive article, we'll explore how designers can harness the power of workspaces and layouts to tailor their Corel Draw experience to diverse design needs.

The Essence of Workspaces and Layouts

Workspaces and layouts in Corel Draw are more than just arrangements of tools and panels. They are dynamic environments that adapt to the designer's task at hand. Whether you're working on a logo, a poster, a website design, or an illustration, creating a workspace that aligns with the requirements of that project streamlines your workflow and optimizes your efficiency.

Creating Workspaces for Specific Tasks

Each design project demands a distinct set of tools and panels. A logo designer might prioritize precision tools and color swatches, while a web designer may need access to grids and layout guides. Corel Draw caters to these diverse needs by allowing designers to create workspaces tailored to specific tasks. By selecting the panels and tools that are relevant to your project, you can eliminate clutter and focus solely on the tools that matter, enhancing your concentration and creativity.

Transitioning Seamlessly Between Projects

Designers often work on multiple projects simultaneously or switch between projects frequently. The ability to switch between different workspaces at a moment's notice ensures a smooth transition. If you were working on a website design and need to suddenly switch to a vector illustration, Corel Draw lets you activate the appropriate workspace with a few clicks. This eliminates the need to manually rearrange panels and tools, saving you time and preventing disruption to your creative flow.

Preserving Customizations for Future Use

Once you've meticulously crafted a workspace that caters to your design needs, Corel Draw allows you to save it for future use. This feature is especially valuable if you have a consistent design style or frequently recurring projects. Over time, you can build a library of customized workspaces, each ready to be activated when needed. This not only enhances your efficiency but also maintains a level of design consistency across various projects.

Choosing Pre-designed Workspaces for Inspiration

For those seeking inspiration or a quick starting point, Corel Draw offers pre-designed workspaces tailored to specific design disciplines. Whether you're working on illustration, typography, photo editing, or UI/UX design, these pre-designed workspaces provide a framework that incorporates relevant tools and panels. You can then modify these layouts to match your personal preferences, creating a hybrid workspace that aligns with your unique workflow.

The Flexibility of Layouts

While workspaces focus on the arrangement of tools and panels, layouts in Corel Draw deal with the structure of your canvas. Designers often require different page sizes and orientations for various projects. Whether you're designing a business card, a poster, or a brochure, Corel Draw's layout options allow you to define custom page sizes, orientations, and even multiple pages within a single document.

Conclusion

The beauty of Corel Draw's workspaces and layouts lies in their adaptability. Designers no longer need to adjust to the software; instead, the software adjusts to them. This level of customization enhances creativity, promotes efficiency, and empowers designers to navigate seamlessly between different design needs. From custom-tailored workspaces that prioritize specific tools to layout options that accommodate diverse projects, Corel Draw's workspaces and layouts empower designers to truly own their creative process. Whether you're crafting intricate vector art or designing a user interface, these features ensure that Corel Draw adapts to your needs, allowing you to focus on what you do best—designing with excellence and innovation.

Chapter 2: Mastering Vector Illustration Techniques

ADVANCED SHAPE MANIPULATION USING NODE EDITING

In the realm of graphic design, the ability to create intricate and custom shapes is a hallmark of expertise. While basic shapes and tools serve as building blocks, it's the manipulation of these elements that truly brings a design to life. Corel Draw, a powerful design software, offers designers a sophisticated toolset for advanced shape manipulation through node editing. In this comprehensive article, we will delve into the world of node editing, exploring how it empowers designers to craft intricate designs with precision and creativity.

Understanding Nodes: The Building Blocks of Shapes

At the heart of Corel Draw's node editing lies a simple yet profound concept—nodes. Nodes are anchor points that define the curvature and structure of vector shapes. These points, when connected, form paths that ultimately shape the design elements. By manipulating these nodes, designers can transform basic shapes into complex and captivating forms.

The Node Editing Interface: Precision at Your Fingertips

Node editing in Corel Draw offers an intuitive interface that allows designers to exercise precision and creativity simultaneously. The Node tool, a fundamental component of the software, serves as the gateway to this realm of shape manipulation. When selected, it reveals the nodes and control handles that define the shape's contours.

Bézier Curves: Sculpting with Control

Bézier curves are the cornerstone of advanced shape manipulation in Corel Draw. These curves, defined by nodes and control handles, provide unparalleled control over the shape's curves and angles. By adjusting the position and orientation of nodes and handles, designers can sculpt shapes to match their artistic vision. This level of control allows for the creation of organic and complex forms that transcend basic geometric shapes.

Creating Smooth Curves with Control Handles

Control handles, often represented as direction lines extending from nodes, dictate the direction and curvature of Bézier curves. By manipulating these handles, designers can achieve smooth transitions between nodes, ensuring that curves flow seamlessly. This level of precision is particularly valuable for creating flowing shapes, intricate lettering, and organic illustrations that mimic natural forms.

Corners and Nodes: Customizing Shapes with Precision

Node editing goes beyond smooth curves; it also allows for precise corner manipulation. Designers can choose between smooth nodes, which produce rounded corners, and cusp nodes, which create sharp corners. By adjusting the position of nodes and control handles, designers can tailor the angles and lengths of the curves, resulting in shapes that are uniquely customized.

Complex Shapes and Compositions: The Art of Node Editing

As designers delve deeper into node editing, they discover its potential for creating complex shapes and compositions. By combining multiple nodes, handles, and segments, intricate designs that showcase depth, movement, and dimensionality can be crafted. This level of artistry is evident in everything from decorative ornaments to intricate patterns and elaborate logo designs.

Merging Creativity and Precision

Node editing epitomizes the harmonious marriage of creativity and precision. It empowers designers to visualize and execute their creative ideas with accuracy, offering a level of control that transcends traditional design methods. Whether it's perfecting the curvature of a letterform, replicating the subtleties of natural textures, or crafting intricate patterns, node editing ensures that the designer's creative intent is meticulously realized.

Conclusion

Advanced shape manipulation using node editing in Corel Draw is akin to sculpting with digital clay. It allows designers to transcend the boundaries of basic shapes, delving into a realm where creativity and precision intertwine. Through the manipulation of nodes and control handles, intricate designs emerge, showcasing the designer's mastery over form and aesthetics. Node editing transforms design from a mechanical process into an artistic endeavor, offering a level of customization and intricacy that defines exceptional design work. Whether you're a seasoned professional seeking to elevate your designs or an aspiring artist eager to explore the depths of creative expression, node editing in Corel Draw is a tool that opens doors to a world of endless possibilities.

CREATING COMPLEX VECTOR ARTWORK WITH THE BÉZIER TOOL

In the realm of graphic design, precision and creativity intersect to produce stunning works of art. One tool that exemplifies this synergy is the Bézier tool, a fundamental feature in Corel Draw that empowers designers to craft intricate and complex vector artwork. In this comprehensive article, we'll delve into the art of creating sophisticated designs using the Bézier tool, exploring its capabilities, techniques, and the realm of possibilities it offers.

The Essence of Bézier Curves

At the heart of the Bézier tool lies the concept of Bézier curves—a mathematical representation of smooth and graceful lines. These curves are defined by control points, which designers manipulate to craft elegant and complex shapes. The Bézier tool grants designers a level of control that goes beyond basic shapes, allowing them to create everything from delicate letterforms to intricate illustrations.

Understanding Control Points and Handles

Control points, also known as nodes, are the anchors that define Bézier curves. These points determine the direction, angle, and curvature of the curve segments. Paired with control handles, which extend from the nodes, designers gain the ability to shape curves precisely. By adjusting the length and direction of these handles, the trajectory of the curve can be fine-tuned, leading to smooth transitions and elegant shapes.

Crafting Smooth and Precise Curves

The beauty of the Bézier tool lies in its ability to create smooth and precise curves that mimic natural forms. Whether you're designing organic shapes, intricate lettering, or elaborate patterns, the Bézier tool enables you to achieve curves that flow seamlessly. By placing nodes strategically and adjusting control handles with care, designers can maintain the fluidity of their designs while preserving the accuracy of the curves.

Creating Complex Shapes with Bézier

While the Bézier tool excels at crafting simple curves, its true potential is realized when creating complex shapes. By connecting multiple Bézier curves, designers can form intricate designs that captivate the viewer's eye. Whether you're designing ornate motifs, intricate foliage, or elaborate flourishes, the Bézier tool allows you to break down complex forms into manageable segments, each defined by control points and handles.

Achieving Symmetry and Balance

Symmetry and balance are vital elements in design, and the Bézier tool is a reliable ally in achieving these principles. By carefully mirroring and duplicating curves, designers can create symmetrical elements that add a sense of harmony to their designs. The precision offered by the Bézier tool ensures that each curve aligns flawlessly with its counterpart, resulting in designs that are visually appealing and well-balanced.

Illustration Mastery with Bézier Curves

The Bézier tool shines particularly bright in the realm of vector illustration. Designers can use it to create intricate character designs, elaborate scenes, and captivating compositions. By breaking down complex illustrations into manageable curves and shapes, the Bézier tool allows designers to bring their imaginative visions to life, from the graceful curves of a character's silhouette to the intricate details of a scene's background.

Practicing Patience and Mastery

Mastery of the Bézier tool is an art that requires patience and practice. The more you use it, the more intuitive it becomes. As your muscle memory develops, you'll find yourself creating complex shapes and curves with increasing ease and precision. The journey of mastering the Bézier tool is a testament to the dedication and passion that designers invest in their craft.

Conclusion

The Bézier tool in Corel Draw is a vehicle that transports designers into the realm of artistry and precision. It offers the means to craft complex vector artwork that marries creativity with accuracy. Whether you're sculpting curves for typography, designing intricate illustrations, or creating patterns that mesmerize, the Bézier tool empowers you to transform your ideas into visual masterpieces. By embracing its capabilities and exploring its nuances, designers unlock a world of creative expression where the marriage of form and function brings designs to life in ways that captivate and inspire.

WORKING WITH LAYERS AND OBJECT MANAGEMENT FOR ORGANIZED DESIGNS

In the realm of graphic design, organization is the bedrock upon which creativity flourishes. A well-structured design not only enhances efficiency but also elevates the quality of the final product. Corel Draw, a versatile design software, offers designers a powerful toolkit for managing complexity through layers and object management. In this comprehensive article, we will explore the art of working with layers and object management, uncovering how these features contribute to organized and visually impactful designs.

Understanding Layers: The Blueprint of Your Design

Layers in Corel Draw function much like transparent sheets, allowing designers to create and organize different elements of a design independently. These elements, whether shapes, text, or images, can be stacked and manipulated individually within their respective layers. This hierarchical approach provides a clear visual structure for complex designs, facilitating ease of editing and enhancing collaboration.

Creating a Visual Hierarchy

A well-organized design communicates information effectively. Layers play a crucial role in establishing a visual hierarchy, where elements are arranged according to their significance. Designers can use layers to group related objects together, ensuring that important elements stand out while maintaining a harmonious balance. For instance, a web design might have separate layers for header, content, and footer, allowing for focused editing and streamlined revisions.

Streamlining Edits and Revisions

Imagine the scenario where a design needs tweaking, but locating the specific element to edit becomes a tedious task. Layers in Corel Draw eliminate this challenge. By compartmentalizing design elements into layers, designers can swiftly locate and modify specific components without affecting the rest of the design. This streamlines the editing process and prevents unintended changes, saving valuable time and effort.

Enhancing Collaboration and Flexibility

In collaborative design projects, layers become a conduit for efficient teamwork. Different team members can work on specific layers, allowing simultaneous progress without interference. Moreover, layers can be easily turned on or off, making it possible to present alternative versions of a design. Whether it's a logo with variations or a layout with multiple options, layers enable designers to showcase creative possibilities while maintaining an organized workflow.

Object Management: Fine-Tuning Design Elements

Object management in Corel Draw takes organization a step further by providing tools for precise control over individual design elements. The Object Manager docker allows designers to view and arrange objects across different layers, providing a bird's-eye view of the composition. This feature is particularly valuable when working on intricate designs that involve numerous elements.

Grouping and Arrangement for Orderly Designs

Corel Draw empowers designers to group objects within layers, ensuring that related elements stay together. This feature is especially beneficial when dealing with design components that need to maintain their relative positions. Designers can group elements to create intricate patterns, arrange complex compositions, or simply ensure that objects stay aligned during design adjustments.

Using Blend Modes for Creative Effects

Blend modes are another tool in Corel Draw's object management arsenal. These modes allow designers to control how one object interacts with another, enabling creative effects such as overlays, transparencies, and shadows. By exploring blend modes within layers, designers can add depth, dimension, and visual interest to their designs.

Conclusion

Working with layers and object management in Corel Draw is akin to crafting an organized symphony of design elements. By strategically using layers to compartmentalize and arrange design components, designers can create a visual hierarchy that enhances communication and navigation. Object management further refines this structure, offering tools for precision and creative manipulation. Whether you're working on a logo, a poster, or a comprehensive design project, the art of layer management and object arrangement ensures that your designs not only captivate the eye but also exemplify the elegance of organized creativity.

Chapter 3: Harnessing the Power of Typography

FINE-TUNING TEXT USING ADVANCED FORMATTING OPTIONS

Typography is an art that wields tremendous influence in the world of graphic design. Beyond conveying information, text can evoke emotions, create atmosphere, and establish visual hierarchy. Corel Draw, a powerful design software, empowers designers to go beyond basic text formatting through its advanced typography tools. In this comprehensive article, we will explore the realm of fine-tuning text using Corel Draw's advanced formatting options, uncovering how they allow designers to shape text into a potent visual element.

Typography as Visual Communication

Typography isn't merely about selecting a font and adjusting its size. It's a means of visual communication that demands precision and artistry. Corel Draw's advanced formatting options recognize this complexity, offering designers a toolkit to refine typography and create text that resonates with audiences on multiple levels.

Fine-Tuning Character Attributes

At the heart of advanced text formatting lies the ability to fine-tune character attributes. Corel Draw allows designers to manipulate character spacing, baseline shift, and even horizontal scaling. This level of control enables the adjustment of text to fit specific design requirements, whether it's aligning text with other elements or creating dynamic text effects.

Kerning and Tracking: Achieving Optical Harmony

Kerning and tracking are pivotal in achieving a harmonious and balanced text appearance. Kerning involves adjusting the spacing between individual letter pairs to optimize visual balance. Tracking, on the other hand, adjusts the overall spacing between all characters in a text block. Corel Draw's advanced typography tools provide designers with the means to achieve optical harmony, ensuring that each letter interacts seamlessly with its neighbors.

Creating Artistic Text Effects

Beyond basic text formatting lies the realm of artistic text effects. Corel Draw's advanced typography options allow designers to warp, bend, and manipulate text, transforming it into an integral part of the design composition. Whether it's curving text along a path, distorting it into shapes, or applying 3D effects, the software's creative possibilities elevate text from static elements to dynamic visual statements.

Integrating Text and Graphics

The synergy between text and graphics can elevate design to a whole new level. Corel Draw facilitates this integration through advanced formatting options that allow text to interact with design elements. Whether you're filling text with images, blending it seamlessly into backgrounds, or creating text masks, Corel Draw empowers designers to weave text into the fabric of the design, enhancing its impact.

Typography in Layout Design

Advanced text formatting is particularly valuable in layout design, where text and imagery need to coexist harmoniously. Corel Draw's text wrap feature allows designers to flow text around images and other design elements, ensuring that the layout remains visually pleasing and easily comprehensible. This is especially useful for projects like magazines, brochures, and web designs.

Fine-Tuning for Branding and Identity

For branding and identity design, consistency is key. Corel Draw's advanced formatting options enable designers to create character and paragraph styles that can be applied consistently across different materials. This ensures that the brand's visual identity remains intact, whether it's on business cards, banners, or digital platforms.

Conclusion

Fine-tuning text using advanced formatting options in Corel Draw is a journey into the heart of typographic creativity. It's about manipulating letters and words to convey not just information, but emotion, atmosphere, and intention. By mastering the art of character spacing, kerning, tracking, and integrating text with design elements, designers can transform text into a dynamic visual element that engages, informs, and captivates. Whether you're creating logos, posters, or typographic art, Corel Draw's advanced typography tools empower you to shape text into a potent design component that speaks volumes in every stroke and curve.

CREATING CUSTOM TEXT EFFECTS AND ARTISTIC TYPOGRAPHY

Typography is more than just words on a page; it's a visual art form that allows designers to convey meaning, emotion, and style. Corel Draw, a versatile design software, offers a rich palette of tools and features that enable designers to push the boundaries of typographic creativity. In this comprehensive article, we will explore the exciting realm of creating custom text effects and artistic typography using Corel Draw, revealing how designers can transform ordinary text into extraordinary visual statements.

The Transformative Power of Custom Text Effects

Custom text effects are the gateway to unlocking the full expressive potential of typography. They allow designers to bend, shape, and mold text into forms that captivate the eye and communicate on multiple levels. Corel Draw's extensive toolset empowers designers to create custom text effects that range from subtle enhancements to bold and dramatic transformations.

Beyond the Basics: Text on a Path

Corel Draw enables designers to break free from the confines of horizontal text. Text on a path is a feature that allows text to follow the contour of a drawn path, resulting in dynamic and visually engaging compositions. Whether you're creating circular logos, curving text around shapes, or designing intricate patterns, text on a path injects an element of movement and creativity into your typography.

Distortion and Warping: Shaping Text with Artistry

Distortion and warping are tools that designers can wield to give text a unique and artistic flair. Corel Draw's envelope distortion tools let you bend, twist, and warp text, creating effects that mimic the texture of fabric, the flow of water, or the contours of a three-dimensional surface. This level of manipulation allows designers to transform text into a canvas for creativity, infusing it with a sense of dynamism and depth.

Depth and Dimension: 3D Text Effects

Corel Draw's 3D text effects elevate typography from the flatness of the page to the realm of immersive depth. Designers can extrude text, giving it volume and presence, and apply lighting and shading effects that create realistic 3D appearances. This technique is especially impactful for creating eye-catching titles, logos, and headings that demand attention and convey a sense of sophistication.

Texturing and Layering: Adding Visual Interest

Texturing and layering are techniques that infuse typography with tactile and visual richness. Corel Draw allows designers to overlay textures onto text, giving it the appearance of materials like wood, metal, or fabric. This level of detail adds depth and authenticity to the design, enhancing its visual appeal and creating a multisensory experience for the viewer.

Integration with Graphics: Creating Harmonious Compositions

Artistic typography shines brightest when integrated seamlessly with graphics and design elements. Corel Draw empowers designers to integrate text with images, illustrations, and shapes to create compositions that are both cohesive and captivating. Whether it's filling text with images or blending it into backgrounds, this integration elevates typography from a standalone element to an integral part of the design narrative.

Expressing Emotion through Typography

Artistic typography isn't just about aesthetics; it's about emotion and storytelling. The choice of fonts, colors, and effects can convey a wide spectrum of emotions, from elegance and sophistication to playfulness and boldness. By experimenting with custom text effects, designers can amplify the emotional impact of their designs, creating typographic compositions that resonate deeply with the audience.

Mastering the Fusion of Art and Typography

Creating custom text effects and artistic typography in Corel Draw is a journey into the fusion of art and design. It's about pushing the boundaries of typographic expression and transforming text into a canvas for creativity. Through distortion, texture, layering, and integration with graphics, designers can craft typographic compositions that transcend the ordinary and become vehicles for artistic communication. Whether you're designing for print, web, or multimedia, Corel Draw's robust toolkit empowers you to wield typography as a powerful artistic medium, creating designs that leave a lasting impression and tell a visual story like no other.

HANDLING TEXT ALONG PATHS AND WITHIN SHAPES

Typography is a visual language that speaks volumes in design, and the way text is positioned can profoundly impact the overall composition. Corel Draw, a versatile design software, equips designers with the tools to manipulate text along paths and within shapes, enabling them to craft engaging and dynamic layouts. In this comprehensive article, we will explore the art of handling text along paths and within shapes in Corel Draw, uncovering how these techniques breathe life into typography and design.

Text on a Path: Curving Typography with Elegance

Text on a path is a creative technique that allows designers to arrange text along a drawn path, adding a layer of fluidity and visual interest. Corel Draw's intuitive interface makes this process seamless, allowing designers to transform ordinary text into captivating compositions. Whether you're designing logos that wrap around circular elements or crafting artistic headlines with a dynamic flow, text on a path adds a touch of elegance and movement to your designs.

Creating Text on a Path: A Step-by-Step Guide

Draw the Path: Begin by drawing the path using any of Corel Draw's drawing tools, such as the Pen tool. The path can be a simple curve or a more intricate shape, depending on your design vision.

Add the Text: Select the Text tool and click along the path where you want the text to start. As you type, the text will automatically follow the contour of the path.

Adjust Alignment: Corel Draw offers options to align the text to the path, both on the inside and outside. Experiment with these alignments to achieve the desired visual effect.

Fine-Tuning: You can further fine-tune the positioning, spacing, and rotation of the text using the Shape tool or the Text tool's formatting options.

Text within Shapes: Merging Typography and Graphics

Designers often seek ways to integrate text seamlessly with graphics and shapes. Corel Draw's ability to place text within shapes achieves this fusion, resulting in visually harmonious compositions. By nesting text inside shapes, designers create designs that are not only cohesive but also convey a deeper layer of meaning and intention.

Steps to Place Text within Shapes

Create the Shape: Begin by creating the shape using Corel Draw's shape tools, such as rectangles, circles, or custom shapes.

Add the Text: Select the Text tool and click inside the shape where you want the text to appear. Type your text, and it will automatically adjust to fit the shape.

Adjust Fit and Alignment: Corel Draw provides options to adjust how the text fits within the shape, such as fitting to the width or height. Additionally, you can align the text within the shape to achieve the desired balance.

Styling and Effects: Explore text formatting options, such as font choice, size, color, and effects, to enhance the visual impact of the design.

Unlocking Visual Impact and Narrative Depth

Handling text along paths and within shapes in Corel Draw isn't just about aesthetics; it's about creating designs that engage and intrigue. The visual impact of text on a path adds movement and elegance, turning words into visual journeys. Placing text within shapes, on the other hand, integrates typography with graphics to tell a more cohesive and nuanced story.

Visual Hierarchy and Emphasis

Text along paths and within shapes offer opportunities to establish visual hierarchy and emphasis. For instance, a curved text path can draw attention to a specific element in a design, while text within a shape can emphasize key messages or enhance the overall narrative.

Narrative and Design Harmony

The fusion of text and shapes goes beyond aesthetics; it enhances the narrative and design harmony. By aligning text with the contours of shapes or embedding it within them, designers create a sense of unity that reinforces the message or theme of the design.

Conclusion

Handling text along paths and within shapes in Corel Draw is a masterful way to infuse typography with creativity and meaning. Whether you're seeking elegant curves that captivate the eye or integrating text seamlessly with design elements, these techniques empower designers to craft compositions that stand out and tell compelling stories. Through the interplay of text and visual elements, Corel Draw's tools facilitate the transformation of typography into a dynamic and integral part of the design process, elevating the visual impact and narrative depth of your creations.

Chapter 4: Beyond the Basics: Advanced Drawing and Design Techniques

EXPLORING GRADIENT MESH FOR REALISTIC SHADING AND HIGHLIGHTS

Graphic design is a canvas for creativity, where visual elements come to life through colors, shapes, and textures. Corel Draw, a versatile design software, offers designers a powerful tool known as the gradient mesh. This tool allows for the creation of intricate, multi-color gradients that simulate realistic shading and highlights, adding depth and dimension to designs. In this comprehensive article, we will delve into the art of exploring gradient mesh in Corel Draw, unveiling how it elevates design by infusing it with the subtleties of light and shadow.

Understanding Gradient Mesh: Painting with Color Transitions

A gradient mesh is a mesh of intersecting lines that form a grid within an object or shape. Each intersection point, known as a mesh point, can be assigned a specific color or transparency value. The result is a smooth transition of colors across the shape, creating the illusion of depth, texture, and dimensionality. By manipulating the colors of individual mesh points, designers can achieve effects that closely resemble natural lighting conditions.

Creating Realistic Shading with Gradient Mesh: A Step-by-Step Guide

Select the Object: Choose the object or shape that you want to apply the gradient mesh to. This could be anything from a simple geometric shape to a more complex illustration.

Apply the Gradient Mesh: With the object selected, navigate to the "Object" menu and choose "Blend." From the submenu, select "Make." A mesh will be applied to the object, with a default set of mesh points.

Adjust Mesh Points: Use the Mesh tool to manipulate the mesh points. Select a mesh point and choose a color from the color palette. Apply darker shades to areas that should be in shadow and lighter shades to areas that should be highlighted.

Create Color Transitions: To achieve smooth color transitions, select neighboring mesh points and adjust their colors accordingly. Use the Eyedropper tool to sample colors from the object or from reference images for a more realistic effect.

Fine-Tune and Experiment: Continue adjusting the colors of mesh points to achieve the desired shading and highlighting. Experiment with different color combinations to achieve the most realistic and visually appealing results.

Adding Highlights and Depth

Gradient mesh doesn't just create shading; it also adds highlights and depth to designs. By strategically placing light-colored mesh points and adjusting their transparency, designers can simulate the way light interacts with surfaces. This technique is particularly effective for creating the illusion of reflective surfaces, metallic textures, or even glass-like translucency.

Applying Gradient Mesh to Illustrations

Illustrations benefit immensely from gradient mesh. Complex forms, such as human faces, natural landscapes, or intricate objects, can be transformed with subtle shading and highlights that give them a lifelike quality. Whether you're striving for photorealism or a painterly effect, gradient mesh enables you to infuse illustrations with a sense of dimension and vitality.

The Art of Patience and Precision

Working with gradient mesh requires patience and precision. It's a technique that demands attention to detail and a keen eye for color. As designers manipulate individual mesh points and refine color transitions, they embark on a journey of artistic discovery, gradually revealing the nuances of light and shadow that breathe life into their designs.

Conclusion

Exploring gradient mesh in Corel Draw is a journey into the realm of realism and artistic expression. By infusing designs with intricate, multi-color gradients, designers can create the illusion of depth, texture, and dimensionality. From realistic shading that simulates natural light to highlights that add brilliance and reflective surfaces, gradient mesh empowers designers to transcend flat shapes and infuse designs with a touch of visual magic. Whether you're crafting illustrations, logos, or intricate compositions, gradient mesh is a tool that transforms your designs into captivating visual narratives, allowing you to paint with the subtleties of light and shadow on the digital canvas.

BLEND TOOL TECHNIQUES FOR SMOOTH TRANSITIONS AND CREATIVE EFFECTS

Graphic design is a realm where creativity meets precision, and the tools at a designer's disposal can bring their artistic visions to life. One such tool that embodies this blend of creativity and precision is the Blend tool in Corel Draw. With its ability to create seamless transitions between objects and generate mesmerizing visual effects, the Blend tool is an essential element in a designer's toolkit. In this comprehensive article, we'll delve into the world of Blend tool techniques, exploring how it enables smooth transitions and opens the door to a realm of creative possibilities.

Understanding the Blend Tool: A Pathway to Artistry

At its core, the Blend tool is a mechanism that generates a series of intermediate objects between two or more selected objects. These objects can be shapes, lines, or even text. By blending these elements, designers can achieve gradual transitions, intricate patterns, and captivating visual effects. The Blend tool is a bridge between precision and creativity, offering a wide spectrum of applications in design.

Creating Seamless Transitions with the Blend Tool: A Step-by-Step Guide

Select Objects: Begin by selecting the objects you want to blend. These objects can be shapes, lines, or even text. The order of selection determines the direction of the blend.

Access the Blend Tool: Locate the Blend tool in the toolbox and click on it. The Blend Options dialog will appear, offering various settings to control the blend's characteristics.

Choose Blend Steps: In the Blend Options dialog, choose the number of steps between the objects.

More steps result in a smoother transition. Preview the blend to ensure it matches your design intent.

Apply and Adjust: Click "Apply" in the Blend Options dialog to create the blend. The intermediate objects will be generated, creating a seamless transition between the selected objects. You can further adjust the blend's appearance using the Shape tool and other formatting options.

Creating Gradient Blends for Dynamic Effects

The Blend tool's capabilities extend beyond simple object transitions. Designers can leverage gradient blends to create dynamic effects that capture the viewer's attention. By blending two objects with gradient fills, you can achieve a gradual shift of color and texture, adding depth and complexity to your designs.

Creating Complex Patterns and Designs

The Blend tool is a secret weapon for creating complex patterns and intricate designs. By blending multiple objects with varying shapes and colors, you can generate captivating visual motifs that resemble natural textures, fabrics, or even surreal landscapes. This technique is particularly valuable when designing backgrounds, decorative elements, or unique illustrations.

Textured and Artistic Blends

Beyond basic shapes, the Blend tool can be used to create textured and artistic blends. By blending objects with varying transparencies, opacities, and effects, designers can achieve a painterly or ethereal effect. This technique is ideal for creating dreamy backgrounds, abstract compositions, and artistic visualizations.

Animating Transitions and Transformations

The Blend tool isn't limited to static designs; it can also be used to create dynamic animations. By blending objects with incremental changes, designers can produce smooth transitions and transformations that add motion and intrigue to their designs. This technique is especially effective in web design and multimedia projects.

Mastery through Experimentation and Innovation

Mastering the Blend tool requires a willingness to experiment and innovate. Designers can combine various objects, colors, and settings to uncover new and unexpected effects. By pushing the boundaries of the tool, they can breathe life into their designs and discover innovative ways to captivate the viewer's eye.

Conclusion

The Blend tool in Corel Draw is a gateway to a world of smooth transitions and creative effects. From seamless transitions between objects to the creation of intricate patterns and dynamic animations, the Blend tool empowers designers to infuse their designs with depth, texture, and visual allure. By blending precision with creativity, designers can craft compositions that transcend the ordinary and mesmerize the viewer with the fluidity and magic of the visual continuum. Whether you're designing logos, illustrations, or multimedia projects, the Blend tool is your ticket to an artistic journey where innovation meets imagination.

CREATING INTRICATE PATTERNS USING THE PATTERN FILL TOOL

Patterns are the visual tapestries that add texture, depth, and dynamism to designs. Corel Draw, a versatile graphic design software, offers a powerful tool known as the Pattern Fill tool, which enables designers to craft intricate patterns that elevate their creations to new levels of visual richness. In this comprehensive article, we will explore the art of creating intricate patterns using the Pattern Fill tool in Corel Draw, uncovering how this tool allows designers to weave complexity and creativity into their designs.

Understanding the Pattern Fill Tool: Transforming Designs with Texture

The Pattern Fill tool in Corel Draw is a gateway to a world of textures, motifs, and visual interest. This tool allows designers to fill shapes and objects with repetitive patterns, transforming flat surfaces into captivating compositions. By utilizing a library of preset patterns or creating custom patterns, designers can infuse their designs with a sense of intricacy that draws the viewer's eye.

Creating Patterns with the Pattern Fill Tool: A Step-by-Step Guide

Select the Object: Begin by selecting the object or shape you want to fill with a pattern. This could be anything from a simple rectangle to a complex illustration.

Access the Pattern Fill Tool: Locate the Pattern Fill tool in the toolbox and click on it. The Pattern Fill dialog will appear, presenting a variety of pattern options.

Choose a Pattern: Corel Draw provides a range of preset patterns to choose from. These patterns vary in style, from geometric shapes to organic textures. Select a pattern that complements your design intent.

Adjust Scale and Angle: In the Pattern Fill dialog, you can adjust the scale and angle of the pattern to suit your design. Preview the pattern within the object to ensure it aligns with your vision.

Customize Colors: Patterns in Corel Draw can be customized with different colors. You can choose a primary color and secondary color for the pattern, allowing you to adapt it to the overall color scheme of your design.

Create and Apply: Once you're satisfied with the pattern settings, click "OK" in the Pattern Fill dialog to apply the pattern to the selected object.

Crafting Custom Patterns: A Creative Endeavor

While Corel Draw offers a library of preset patterns, the true potential of the Pattern Fill tool shines when designers create their own custom patterns. This process involves crafting intricate motifs and textures that are uniquely tailored to the design at hand. By designing custom patterns, designers can add a personal touch to their creations and ensure that their designs stand out with originality.

Steps to Create Custom Patterns

Design the Motif: Begin by designing the motif that will form the basis of your pattern. This could be a simple geometric shape, a complex illustration, or anything in between.

Group the Motif: Once the motif is designed, group all its elements together. This ensures that the pattern retains its integrity when it's applied repeatedly.

Access the Pattern Fill Tool: Open the Pattern Fill tool and select the option to create a new pattern. Choose the grouped motif as the basis for the pattern.

Define Pattern Parameters: In the Pattern Fill dialog, define the pattern's scale, angle, and color settings. Preview the pattern to ensure that it's aligned as desired.
Save and Apply: After creating the custom pattern, save it for future use. Then, apply the pattern to your design objects, transforming them with your unique creation.

Exploring Creative Possibilities

The Pattern Fill tool offers a realm of creative possibilities that extend beyond mere repetition. Designers can experiment with blending modes, opacity settings, and layer arrangements to achieve intricate compositions that capture attention. By layering patterns, combining shapes, and utilizing masking techniques, designers can create complex visual narratives that showcase their artistic prowess.

Dynamic Backgrounds and Texture

The Pattern Fill tool is a particularly valuable asset when creating dynamic backgrounds and textures. Whether you're designing websites, banners, or print materials, patterns can add visual interest and depth to the background, making the design more engaging and memorable.

Conclusion

The Pattern Fill tool in Corel Draw is a window into the world of intricate patterns that breathe life into designs. Whether you're seeking to add texture, depth, or a touch of creativity, patterns have the power to transform flat surfaces into captivating visual compositions. By utilizing preset patterns, creating custom motifs, and exploring blending options, designers can unleash their creativity and craft designs that resonate with texture and visual allure. From illustrations to branding elements, the Pattern Fill tool is a tool that empowers designers to weave complexity, creativity, and originality into their creations, elevating them from ordinary to extraordinary.

Chapter 5: Masterful Photo Editing and Manipulation

UNDERSTANDING PHOTO EFFECTS: RETOUCHING, ENHANCING, AND CREATIVE EDITS

Photography is a visual language that speaks to the heart and captures moments in time. In the digital age, photo editing has become an integral part of the photography process, allowing photographers and designers to transform images, tell stories, and evoke emotions. From subtle retouching to dramatic creative edits, photo effects play a pivotal role in shaping the narrative of an image. In this comprehensive article, we'll delve into the world of photo effects, exploring retouching, enhancing, and creative edits, and uncovering how they elevate photography and visual storytelling.

Retouching: The Art of Subtle Refinement

Retouching involves refining an image to achieve a polished and seamless appearance. It's about enhancing natural beauty and addressing minor imperfections without altering the essence of the subject. Whether it's removing blemishes, minimizing wrinkles, or adjusting skin tones, retouching is a skill that requires a delicate touch and an eye for detail.

Skin Retouching Techniques

Blemish Removal: Use the healing brush tool to gently remove small imperfections such as pimples, scars, and moles.

Smoothing Skin: Employ the clone stamp tool or the blur tool to achieve smooth skin textures while preserving the natural look.
Enhancing Eyes: Brighten and sharpen the eyes using adjustment layers to bring out their vibrancy and depth.

Teeth Whitening: Use a selective brush to whiten teeth and enhance smiles while maintaining a natural appearance.

Enhancing: Elevating Visual Impact

Enhancing photo effects focus on optimizing an image's color, contrast, and composition to make it more visually striking. This category of effects aims to showcase the subject in the best light possible by emphasizing its features and creating a captivating visual experience.

Color Correction and Balance

White Balance Adjustment: Correct color casts by adjusting the white balance to ensure accurate and natural color representation.

Contrast and Saturation: Enhance contrast and saturation to make colors pop and create a more dynamic visual impact.

Selective Exposure Adjustments: Use gradient filters or adjustment brushes to balance exposure in specific areas of the image.

Creative Edits: Unleashing Artistic Expression

Creative photo effects are where imagination takes flight. These effects go beyond reality to evoke emotions, tell stories, and create visual experiences that leave a lasting impression. Creative edits can transform mundane scenes into surreal landscapes, or emphasize certain aspects of an image to convey a powerful message.

Applying Creative Filters and Textures

Vintage and Film Effects: Apply filters that emulate the look of vintage cameras and films, adding a nostalgic or timeless quality to the image.

Texturizing Effects: Overlay textures or patterns to create a unique and tactile visual experience, giving the image a handmade or painterly feel.

Selective Colorization: Convert an image to black and white while preserving specific elements in color to draw attention and create a focal point.

Double Exposure and Blending: Combine multiple images through blending modes to create surreal and artistic compositions.

The Balance of Art and Technique

Mastering photo effects is a harmonious blend of artistic vision and technical proficiency. Each effect serves a purpose, whether it's enhancing the natural beauty of a portrait, boosting the vibrancy of a landscape, or crafting an imaginative visual narrative. While the tools and techniques are essential, it's the creativity and intent behind each edit that breathes life into the image.

Ethics and Authenticity

As with any art form, photo effects come with ethical considerations. It's important to strike a balance between enhancing an image and maintaining its authenticity. In journalistic and documentary photography, maintaining the integrity of the captured moment is paramount, while in creative and commercial photography, the boundaries are more flexible, allowing for artistic interpretation.

Conclusion

Understanding photo effects encompasses a spectrum of skills, from retouching to enhancing and creative editing. These effects empower photographers and designers to tell stories, evoke emotions, and convey messages through imagery. Whether the goal is to refine the beauty of a subject, elevate visual impact, or unleash artistic expression, photo effects are the brushstrokes that transform raw images into compelling visual narratives. By blending technical expertise with creative ingenuity, photographers and designers shape the way we perceive the world and invite us to explore the rich tapestry of visual storytelling.

WORKING WITH MASKS AND CLIPPING PATHS FOR PRECISE IMAGE CONTROL

Image manipulation is an art form that allows designers and photographers to shape visual narratives with precision and creativity. In this digital age, working with masks and clipping paths has become a fundamental technique for achieving precise image control and seamless integration within designs. These tools enable designers to manipulate elements within an image while preserving the original content, opening doors to limitless creative possibilities. In this comprehensive article, we'll explore the world of masks and clipping paths, uncovering how they empower artists to achieve intricate, refined, and visually captivating compositions.

Understanding Masks and Clipping Paths: Unleashing Creative Potential

Masks and clipping paths are techniques that allow designers to isolate specific parts of an image, control their visibility, and apply various effects while leaving the rest of the image unaffected. These tools are crucial for non-destructive editing, as they preserve the original image data and enable adjustments to be made without permanently altering the pixels.

Layer Masks: Harnessing Flexibility and Control

Layer masks are the cornerstone of non-destructive editing. They act as invisible shields that allow you to reveal or conceal specific parts of a layer. This technique is particularly valuable for seamlessly blending images, combining multiple exposures, or creating composite visuals. By painting on a layer mask with black, white, and varying shades of gray, designers can control the visibility and opacity of different elements within the layer.

Creating a Layer Mask: A Step-by-Step Guide

Select the Layer: Begin by selecting the layer you want to apply the mask to. This could be an image, text, or any other design element.

Add a Layer Mask: Locate the "Add Layer Mask" button at the bottom of the Layers panel and click on it. A white thumbnail will appear next to the layer's thumbnail.

Use the Brush Tool: Select the Brush tool and set the foreground color to black. Paint on the layer mask to hide parts of the layer. To reveal areas, switch the foreground color to white and continue painting.

Refine with Gradients and Opacity: Layer masks can also be refined using gradients and opacity settings. Gradual transitions can be achieved by painting with varying levels of gray.

Clipping Paths: Isolating Elements with Precision

Clipping paths are particularly useful for isolating complex shapes or objects from their backgrounds. This technique involves creating a vector path that acts as a boundary, allowing only the content within the path to be visible. This level of precision is especially beneficial for product photography, where objects need to be presented against a variety of backgrounds.

Creating a Clipping Path: A Step-by-Step Guide

Select the Object: Begin by selecting the object you want to isolate using a clipping path. This could be a product, an illustration, or any other element.
Path Creation: Use the Pen tool or any other vector tool to create a path that outlines the object you want

to keep visible. Ensure the path encloses the object entirely.

Apply the Clipping Path: Once the path is created, go to the "Object" menu and choose "Clipping Path." From the submenu, select "Make." The object within the path will now be isolated.

Unlocking Creative Possibilities

Working with masks and clipping paths goes beyond basic isolation; it offers a gateway to innovative designs and imaginative compositions.

Combining Masks and Clipping Paths: By using layer masks in conjunction with clipping paths, designers can seamlessly integrate objects into new environments while applying intricate adjustments that enhance the final composition.

Creating Artistic Effects: Masks and clipping paths can be used to apply artistic effects such as vignettes, selective focus, or surreal color blends, allowing designers to create images that transcend reality.

Achieving Visual Harmony: Masks and clipping paths contribute to achieving visual harmony by enabling precise control over elements' placement, allowing designers to arrange images and text in visually balanced compositions.

Conclusion

Working with masks and clipping paths in the realm of image manipulation is a journey of artistic control and creative expression. These techniques empower designers and photographers to achieve precision, finesse, and innovation in their work. Whether it's seamlessly blending images, isolating objects, or crafting intricate visual effects, masks and clipping paths are the tools that allow artists to shape their visual narratives with meticulous attention to detail. By embracing these techniques, designers harness the power to create compositions that captivate, resonate, and evoke emotions, all while preserving the integrity of the original imagery.

COMBINING VECTOR AND RASTER ELEMENTS SEAMLESSLY

In the world of design, the marriage of vector and raster elements has given rise to visually captivating compositions that seamlessly blend precision and realism. Whether in digital art, graphic design, or multimedia projects, the harmonious integration of vector and raster elements opens the door to a realm of creativity that transcends traditional boundaries. In this comprehensive article, we will explore the art of combining vector and raster elements seamlessly, uncovering how this fusion of techniques empowers designers to create visually dynamic and emotionally resonant works of art.

Understanding Vector and Raster Elements: The Balance of Precision and Realism

Vector and raster elements represent two distinct forms of digital imagery, each with its own set of attributes and advantages.

Vector Elements: Vector graphics are composed of mathematical paths defined by points and curves. They are infinitely scalable without losing quality, making them ideal for logos, illustrations, and typography. Vector graphics are defined by smooth lines and sharp edges, providing a level of precision that's essential for certain design applications.

Raster Elements: Raster graphics, also known as bitmap images, are composed of pixels arranged on a grid. They excel at representing complex textures, subtle gradients, and photographic realism. Raster images are particularly well-suited for capturing intricate details and conveying emotions through visuals.

Seamlessly Combining Vector and Raster: A Step-by-Step Guide

Combining vector and raster elements involves integrating the best of both worlds to achieve a harmonious visual composition.

Select the Elements: Begin by selecting the vector and raster elements you wish to combine. This could be vector-based text, shapes, or illustrations alongside raster images.

Create a New Document: Open a new document in your preferred design software, such as Adobe Illustrator or Corel Draw.

Place the Raster Image: Import the raster image into the document and position it where you want it to appear in relation to the vector elements.

Rasterize if Necessary: Depending on the software, you may need to rasterize the vector elements to seamlessly integrate them with the raster image. Rasterizing converts vector paths into pixels, allowing them to blend naturally with the raster elements.

Blend Mode and Opacity: Experiment with blend modes and opacity settings to achieve the desired interaction between vector and raster elements. Blend modes control how the two elements interact visually, while adjusting opacity influences their transparency.

Refine and Adjust: Fine-tune the composition by manipulating layers, applying masking techniques, or adjusting color and tone to ensure a seamless integration that achieves the desired visual impact.

Unlocking Creative Possibilities

The fusion of vector and raster elements transcends technicalities, enabling designers to explore new horizons of creativity.

Mixed Media Art: By combining vector illustrations with raster photographs, designers can create mixed media artworks that merge the precision of vector lines with the richness of photographic textures.

Realistic Collages: The combination of vector shapes and raster textures can result in collage-style compositions that evoke a sense of depth, nostalgia, or storytelling.

Dynamic Typography: Integrating vector text with raster images allows designers to create typography that interacts with visuals in ways that are visually striking and conceptually engaging.

Conclusion

The art of seamlessly combining vector and raster elements is a testament to the versatility and power of modern design tools. This fusion bridges the gap between precision and realism, offering designers a canvas for creative expression that knows no boundaries. Whether it's crafting mixed media art, designing realistic collages, or creating dynamic typography, the synergy between vectors and rasters elevates designs to a level of visual complexity that resonates deeply with audiences. By harnessing the strengths of both worlds, designers have the ability to craft compositions that speak to the intellect and emotions, creating visual narratives that leave a lasting impression and tell stories that transcend pixels and paths.

Chapter 6: Dynamic Artwork with Blends, Brushes, and Effects

UTILIZING BLENDS AND CONTOURS FOR DYNAMIC SHAPES AND GRADIENTS

In the realm of digital design, the interplay of shapes and gradients brings a visual symphony to life. The strategic use of blends and contours allows designers to create dynamic compositions that captivate the eye and evoke emotions. Whether in logo design, illustration, or visual storytelling, the fusion of shapes and gradients brings depth, movement, and dimensionality to the forefront. In this comprehensive article, we will explore the art of utilizing blends and contours to craft dynamic shapes and gradients, unveiling how these techniques empower designers to orchestrate visual harmonies that resonate with audiences.

Understanding Blends and Contours: A Dance of Form and Color

Blends and contours are techniques that leverage the relationship between shapes and gradients to achieve stunning visual effects.

Blends: Blending involves the gradual transition between two or more objects, resulting in a smooth morphing effect. Blends are versatile tools that create seamless connections, whether it's a transition from one shape to another or a progression of colors.

Contours: Contours are the outlines or edges of shapes, defining their boundaries. Utilizing contour lines can add depth, structure, and movement to designs, allowing for intricate visual exploration.

Creating Dynamic Shapes with Blends: A Step-by-Step Guide

The blend tool offers designers the ability to create dynamic shapes that seamlessly transition from one form to another.

Select Shapes: Begin by selecting the shapes you want to blend. These shapes could be simple geometric forms, complex illustrations, or even text elements.

Access the Blend Tool: Locate the Blend tool in your design software's toolbox and click on it. The Blend

Options dialog will appear, allowing you to control the blending process.

Choose Blend Steps: In the Blend Options dialog, specify the number of steps for the blend. More steps result in a smoother transition between shapes. Preview the blend to ensure it aligns with your vision.

Apply and Adjust: Click "Apply" in the Blend Options dialog to create the blend. You can further adjust the blend's appearance using the Shape tool or other transformation tools.

Crafting Gradient Contours for Dimensionality: A Visual Symphony

Gradient contours offer a dynamic way to add depth and dimensionality to shapes, allowing designers to create captivating visual effects.

Creating Gradient Contours: A Step-by-Step Guide

Select the Shape: Choose the shape you want to apply a gradient contour to. This could be any vector shape in your design.

Access the Gradient Tool: Locate the Gradient tool in your design software and select the shape. The Gradient tool allows you to apply gradients to specific areas of the shape.

Define the Gradient Contour: Using the Gradient tool, define the contour lines by specifying color stops and adjusting their positions. The gradient will follow the shape's contours, creating a sense of depth and form.

Fine-Tune and Experiment: Play with different gradient contour configurations, color combinations, and opacity settings to achieve the desired visual impact.

Dynamic Integration of Blends and Contours

Combining blends and contours allows designers to create compositions that showcase the fusion of shape and gradient techniques.

Fluid Transitions: Blending between shapes while applying gradient contours creates fluid transitions that visually guide the viewer's eye across the composition.

Organic Forms: Contours can shape gradients to mimic organic forms found in nature, adding a touch of realism and elegance to design elements.

Immersive Visual Journeys: By strategically placing blended shapes with gradient contours, designers can lead viewers on immersive visual journeys that unfold as they explore the composition.

Conclusion

The mastery of blends and contours is a voyage into the realm of form, color, and visual storytelling. These techniques empower designers to orchestrate shapes and gradients in ways that captivate and intrigue. Whether it's crafting dynamic transitions, infusing forms with depth and dimensionality, or guiding the viewer's eye through immersive visual landscapes, the fusion of blends and contours unlocks a symphony of possibilities. By embracing these techniques, designers wield the power to create compositions that transcend the boundaries of the two-dimensional canvas, creating visual narratives that resonate with the viewer's senses and emotions.

DESIGNING CUSTOM BRUSHES FOR UNIQUE ARTISTIC EFFECTS

In the realm of digital design, brushes are more than just tools; they're the strokes of creativity that breathe life into visuals. While software comes equipped with an array of default brushes, the ability to design custom brushes opens the door to a world of unique artistic effects that elevate designs to new heights. Whether in illustration, digital painting, or graphic design, creating custom brushes empowers artists to infuse their creations with a touch of originality and innovation. In this comprehensive article, we will dive into the art of designing custom brushes, uncovering how this process transforms mere tools into channels for artistic expression.

Understanding Custom Brushes: Beyond Default Tools

Custom brushes are a departure from the default brushes that come preloaded in design software. While default brushes are versatile and serve general purposes, custom brushes are tailor-made to achieve specific artistic effects, textures, and styles.

Brush Characteristics to Customize:

Shape: The silhouette of the brush stroke, which can range from organic shapes to geometric forms.

Texture: The surface quality of the brush, ranging from smooth to rough or textured.

Opacity: The transparency of the brush stroke, influencing the intensity of the applied color.

Flow: The rate at which paint is applied, affecting the density of the brush stroke.

Scatter: The distribution of multiple instances of the brush shape, creating a scattered or dispersed effect.

Color Dynamics: The variation in color as the brush is applied, adding realism and depth.

Designing Custom Brushes: A Step-by-Step Guide

Creating custom brushes is a process that involves crafting brush presets that align with your artistic vision.

Conceptualize the Effect: Before designing the brush, have a clear idea of the effect you want to achieve. Whether it's replicating a natural texture, emulating a traditional medium, or creating a unique mark-making tool, having a concept in mind is crucial.

Select a Base Shape: Choose a base shape for your brush. This could be anything from a simple line to a complex pattern.

Apply Texture and Dynamics: Customize the brush's texture, opacity, flow, scatter, and color dynamics to achieve the desired effect. Experiment with settings until the brush behaves the way you envision.

Save as a Custom Brush: Once the brush is designed, save it as a custom brush preset in your software. This allows you to reuse the brush in different projects.

Unlocking Creative Potential with Custom Brushes

The use of custom brushes transcends mere tool manipulation, offering a canvas for innovation and artistic exploration.

Textural Realism: Custom brushes can mimic the textures of traditional artistic mediums, adding a layer of authenticity to digital creations.

Expressive Mark Making: Brushes with unique shapes and dynamics enable artists to create expressive mark-making techniques that evoke emotions and energy.

Distinctive Styles: Custom brushes allow artists to develop signature styles that set their work apart, whether through intricate patterns, subtle details, or bold strokes.

Conclusion

Designing custom brushes is an avenue for artists to transform digital tools into instruments of artistic expression. It's a process that bridges the gap between technology and creativity, allowing artists to shape their visions with precision and originality. Whether it's replicating the look of traditional mediums, achieving distinctive textures, or creating bold and expressive marks, custom brushes empower artists to craft visuals that resonate deeply with viewers. By embracing the art of custom brush design, designers and illustrators wield brushes that aren't just tools; they're pathways to creative ingenuity and unique visual narratives that leave a lasting impression.

APPLYING AND CUSTOMIZING SPECIAL EFFECTS FOR EYE-CATCHING DESIGNS

In the realm of design, special effects are the secret ingredients that transform ordinary visuals into extraordinary works of art. These effects add depth, intrigue, and visual allure, capturing the viewer's attention and leaving a lasting impression. From subtle enhancements to dramatic flourishes, special effects are the brushstrokes that infuse designs with a touch of magic. In this comprehensive article, we will delve into the art of applying and customizing special effects, unveiling how these techniques empower designers to craft eye-catching and captivating designs that resonate with audiences.

Understanding Special Effects: Elevating Design to New Heights

Special effects encompass a range of techniques that enhance the visual impact of designs, creating captivating compositions that stand out in a crowded visual landscape.

Types of Special Effects:

Light and Shadow Effects: Techniques that replicate how light interacts with objects, creating realistic shadows, highlights, and reflections.

Textural Effects: Methods that add tactile depth to designs, simulating surfaces like wood, metal, fabric, or glass.

Glow and Glitter Effects: Effects that mimic the shimmer and glow of light sources, adding an ethereal and enchanting quality.

Distortion and Blur Effects: Techniques that alter the perception of depth and motion, creating dynamic and surreal visual experiences.

Applying Special Effects: A Step-by-Step Guide

Applying special effects involves a blend of technical know-how and creative intuition to achieve the desired visual impact.

Identify the Design Element: Begin by selecting the design element you want to enhance with a special effect. This could be text, an image, an illustration, or a background.

Access Special Effect Tools: Different design software offers various tools for applying special effects. Locate tools or features that align with the effect you have in mind.

Configure Effect Settings: Adjust the settings to achieve the desired effect intensity, size, color, and placement. Preview the effect in real time to ensure it matches your vision.

Fine-Tune and Refine: Experiment with different settings, blending modes, and opacity levels to achieve the perfect balance between the effect and the rest of the design.

Customizing Special Effects for Unique Visual Narratives

While applying predefined special effects can yield captivating results, customizing these effects allows designers to infuse their work with a touch of originality and personal style.

Color Customization: Adjust the color palette of the special effect to match the overall design scheme or evoke specific emotions.

Layering and Blending: Combine multiple special effects with various blending modes to create intricate visual textures and harmonious compositions.

Masking and Opacity: Utilize masking techniques to apply special effects to specific areas, creating focal points and guiding the viewer's eye.

Animating Effects: In multimedia projects, animating special effects can bring designs to life, adding a dynamic dimension to the visual narrative.

Achieving the Wow Factor

The strategic application and customization of special effects can elevate designs to new heights, capturing attention and creating memorable impressions.

Visual Hierarchy: Special effects can be used to establish visual hierarchy by drawing the viewer's eye to specific elements within the design.

Storytelling: By applying effects that enhance mood and atmosphere, designers can create designs that tell compelling stories and evoke emotional responses.

Branding and Identity: Special effects can become signature elements that reinforce a brand's identity, making designs instantly recognizable.

Conclusion

The art of applying and customizing special effects is a journey of creativity and technical mastery. It's a fusion of art and technology that transforms designs into visual masterpieces that resonate with audiences. Whether it's crafting realistic textures, adding a touch of magic with glowing effects, or distorting reality for surreal compositions, special effects are the tools that designers wield to captivate and enchant. By embracing these techniques, designers unlock the potential to create designs that go beyond aesthetics, leaving a lasting impression, telling stories, and igniting emotions in the hearts and minds of viewers.

Chapter 7: Professional Print and Digital Output
PREPARING DESIGNS FOR PRINT: CMYK, DPI, AND COLOR MANAGEMENT

The transition from screen to paper is a pivotal moment in the life of a design. As digital creations make their way to print, a set of fundamental considerations come into play to ensure the fidelity, accuracy, and visual impact of the final product. Among these considerations, understanding the nuances of CMYK color space, DPI (dots per inch), and color management stands as a key pillar in the realm of preparing designs for print. In this comprehensive article, we will delve into the intricacies of these elements, unveiling how designers navigate CMYK, DPI, and color management to create print materials that capture attention and convey their intended message with precision.

Understanding CMYK Color Space: The Shift from RGB to Print

CMYK (Cyan, Magenta, Yellow, Key/Black) color space is specifically tailored for print production. Unlike the

RGB (Red, Green, Blue) color space, which is used for digital screens, CMYK accounts for the subtractive nature of ink on paper. As a result, designs need to be converted from RGB to CMYK to ensure accurate color representation in the final printed piece.

RGB to CMYK Conversion: A Necessity for Print

Color Shifts: During the RGB to CMYK conversion, colors might shift due to the differences in color gamuts between the two color spaces. Vibrant and saturated RGB colors may appear slightly muted in CMYK.

Calibration and Profiling: The accuracy of color conversion relies on proper monitor calibration and color profiling of printers to ensure consistency between the on-screen appearance and the printed output.

DPI: The Resolution Game

DPI, or dots per inch, refers to the number of individual dots that make up an inch of an image. This metric determines the level of detail and sharpness in the printed output. Designing with the correct DPI is crucial to avoid pixelation and achieve high-quality print materials.

Print Resolution Standards:

300 DPI: The industry standard for high-quality print materials such as brochures, posters, and magazines. This resolution ensures crisp and detailed images.

150 DPI: Suitable for large-format prints like banners and billboards, where viewing distance allows for a lower DPI without compromising image quality.

Color Management: Bridging the Digital-to-Print Gap

Color management is a meticulous process that ensures consistent color reproduction across various devices, from screen to printer. It involves creating color profiles for monitors and printers, and using software to ensure accurate color translation from screen to print.

Color Calibration and Profiling:

Monitor Calibration: Adjusting your monitor's settings to ensure accurate color representation. Calibration tools and software are used to achieve consistent colors.

Printer Profiling: Creating profiles that define how colors will appear when printed using a specific printer and paper combination. This minimizes color discrepancies between what's seen on screen and what's printed.

Embracing Color Accuracy and Consistency

The journey from designing on screen to delivering the final printed product demands meticulous attention to detail in terms of color accuracy and consistency.

Proofing: Before sending a design to print, create a proof to preview how the design will look on paper. This step helps identify potential color issues and allows for adjustments.

Color Swatches: Utilize Pantone color swatches for precise color reproduction, especially when branding requires consistent colors across different materials.

Communication: Establish open communication with print professionals to ensure a clear understanding of color expectations and technical requirements.

Conclusion

Preparing designs for print is a process that demands a keen understanding of CMYK color space, DPI, and color management. These elements ensure that the visual intent of a design is faithfully translated from screen to paper, resulting in high-quality and impactful printed materials. By mastering the nuances of CMYK conversion, selecting appropriate DPI, and implementing effective color management practices, designers bridge the gap between digital creativity and tangible results. In this convergence of technology and craftsmanship, designers have the power to deliver print materials that resonate with audiences, leaving a lasting impression that captures the essence of their creative vision.

EXPORTING FOR WEB AND DIGITAL MEDIA WITH OPTIMAL SETTINGS

In the dynamic realm of digital design, the process of exporting files for web and digital media plays a critical role in ensuring that your creations shine with the same brilliance online as they do on your screen. With the ever-evolving landscape of devices, platforms, and user expectations, understanding and applying optimal export settings is essential for delivering visually appealing and fast-loading content. In this comprehensive article, we will explore the intricacies of exporting for web and digital media, uncovering how designers master the art of striking a balance between visual quality and efficient delivery.

Understanding the Digital Landscape: Devices, Platforms, and Formats

Before diving into export settings, it's essential to grasp the diversity of devices and platforms your digital content will be consumed on.

Responsive Design: Ensure that your designs are responsive, adapting seamlessly to various screen sizes and orientations, from desktop monitors to smartphones and tablets.

Web Platforms: Consider the platforms your content will appear on, such as websites, social media, and multimedia platforms. Each platform may have specific requirements for file sizes and formats.

Image Formats: Familiarize yourself with common image formats used online, including JPEG, PNG, GIF, and SVG. Each format has its strengths and is suited for specific types of content.

Optimal Export Settings: Striking a Balance

The optimal export settings for web and digital media depend on factors such as the content's purpose, the platform it will be published on, and the desired balance between visual quality and file size.

Resolution and DPI: Web images are typically displayed at a resolution of 72 DPI (dots per inch). This resolution strikes a balance between image clarity and file size, ensuring fast loading times.

JPEG Compression: JPEG is the go-to format for photographs and images with complex color gradients. Adjust the compression level to find the right balance between visual quality and file size.

PNG Compression: PNG is ideal for images with transparency, solid colors, and text. Choose between PNG-8 (for simpler graphics) and PNG-24 (for images with a broader color range).

GIF for Animation: GIFs are suitable for short animations and simple graphics. Opt for a limited color palette and consider looping options.

SVG for Scalability: SVG is perfect for graphics that need to be scalable without loss of quality, such as icons and logos. It's especially useful for responsive designs.

File Size Considerations: Faster Load Times, Better User Experience

As users demand faster load times, the size of your exported files plays a crucial role in optimizing the user experience.

Compress Images: Utilize image compression tools and software to reduce file sizes without significant loss of visual quality.

Minimize Code: If your content includes code (HTML, CSS, JavaScript), ensure it's clean and optimized to prevent unnecessary bloat.

Consider Lazy Loading: For websites with a lot of images, consider implementing lazy loading techniques to load images only as users scroll down, reducing initial load times.

Testing and Iteration: Fine-Tuning Export Settings

Before finalizing your export settings, thorough testing across different devices, platforms, and browsers is crucial.

Responsive Testing: Use responsive design testing tools to preview how your content appears on various devices and orientations.

Browser Compatibility: Test your exported content on multiple browsers to ensure consistent rendering and performance.

Load Time Evaluation: Analyze load times using performance testing tools. Aim for load times that keep users engaged and prevent them from bouncing due to slow loading.

Conclusion

Exporting for web and digital media is a blend of technical finesse and creative intent. By understanding the digital landscape, choosing optimal export settings, and testing across various platforms, designers ensure that their creations are presented with the highest visual quality and fast loading times. In this pursuit of excellence, designers craft digital experiences that captivate users, convey messages effectively, and leave a lasting impression. The synergy of design acumen and technical mastery shines in the ability to export content that not only delights the eyes but also offers a seamless and immersive journey in the digital realm.

TIPS FOR COLLABORATING WITH PRINTERS AND OTHER PROFESSIONALS

In the dynamic world of design, collaboration is the cornerstone of turning creative visions into tangible realities. Whether you're working with printers, photographers, copywriters, or other professionals, effective collaboration is a skill that can elevate your projects from good to exceptional. The synergy between design expertise and seamless teamwork can result in creations that resonate deeply with audiences and leave a lasting impact. In this comprehensive article, we will explore invaluable tips for collaborating with printers and other professionals, uncovering how to forge relationships that foster creativity, efficiency, and successful outcomes.

Understanding the Importance of Collaboration

Collaboration is the glue that binds together the diverse elements of a project. When you collaborate effectively with printers and other professionals, you tap into a wealth of expertise that can enhance your design, streamline the production process, and ensure the final product aligns with your creative vision.

Clear Communication: Open and transparent communication is the foundation of successful collaboration. Clearly convey your ideas, expectations, and project requirements.

Leveraging Expertise: Professionals in different fields bring unique insights to the table. Embrace their expertise to elevate your project and push boundaries.

Building Relationships: Strong professional relationships lead to more fruitful collaborations. Establishing rapport and trust fosters a positive working environment.

Working with Printers: Key Insights

Collaborating with printers is a pivotal aspect of bringing your digital designs to life in print form. The printer-designer partnership requires careful coordination to ensure that your vision translates seamlessly onto physical materials.

Understand Print Requirements: Familiarize yourself with the printer's specifications, including color profiles, bleed settings, and paper choices. This minimizes potential issues during the printing process.

Provide High-Quality Assets: Deliver print-ready files with high-resolution images, proper color modes (CMYK), and appropriate file formats (PDF, TIFF, etc.).

Proofing and Testing: Request proofs to ensure that colors, layouts, and overall presentation meet your expectations before mass production begins.

Collaborating with Other Professionals: Harmonizing Expertise

Beyond printers, collaborations with photographers, copywriters, and other professionals can amplify the impact of your projects.

Copywriters: Collaborating with copywriters ensures that the written content complements your design and resonates with the intended audience.

Photographers: Effective communication with photographers ensures that images align with your design vision, and the tone and style of visuals match the project's aesthetic.

Web Developers: When working on digital projects, collaborating with web developers ensures that your designs are faithfully translated into functional websites or applications.

Tips for Seamless Collaboration

Establish Clear Objectives: Define project goals, timelines, and expectations from the outset to ensure everyone is on the same page.

Regular Communication: Maintain open lines of communication throughout the collaboration, providing updates, feedback, and addressing concerns promptly.

Respect and Value Expertise: Acknowledge and respect the contributions of your collaborators. Their insights can bring fresh perspectives and innovation to your project.

Feedback Loop: Encourage constructive feedback and be receptive to suggestions. A healthy feedback loop enhances the quality of the end product.

Problem-Solving Mindset: Challenges can arise during collaborations. Approach these challenges with a problem-solving mindset and a willingness to find mutually beneficial solutions.

Conclusion

Collaborating with printers and other professionals is a dance of creativity, expertise, and teamwork. By understanding the unique contributions each professional brings to the table, fostering clear communication, and valuing the power of collaboration, designers can elevate their projects to new heights. The seamless integration of diverse talents and skills results in designs that not only capture attention but also convey messages effectively, leaving an indelible impression on audiences. Through the art of collaboration, designers unleash the full potential of their creativity, crafting works that resonate, inspire, and stand as a testament to the power of collective ingenuity.

Chapter 8: Time-Saving Techniques for Efficient Workflows

CREATING TEMPLATES AND STYLES FOR CONSISTENT DESIGN AESTHETICS

Consistency is the cornerstone of effective design—a cohesive visual language that guides the viewer's journey and conveys a brand's identity with precision. In the realm of digital design, creating templates and styles is a powerful approach to achieving this consistency. These tools act as the blueprint for your design projects, ensuring a harmonious and uniform aesthetic that resonates across various materials and platforms. In this comprehensive article, we will delve into the art of creating templates and styles, uncovering how designers wield these tools to craft visual narratives that leave a lasting impression.

Understanding Templates and Styles: The Pillars of Consistency

Templates: Design templates are pre-designed layouts that serve as a foundation for various materials, such as brochures, presentations, social media graphics, and websites. They streamline the design process, providing a structured framework that can be customized with specific content.

Styles: Design styles encompass the visual elements that define a brand's identity. This includes typography, color palettes, imagery, icons, and other design elements. Consistent use of these styles creates a recognizable and cohesive look across all materials.

Benefits of Templates and Styles:

Consistency: Templates and styles ensure that design elements are used consistently across all materials, reinforcing brand identity and improving user experience.

Efficiency: Design templates save time by providing a starting point, allowing designers to focus on content creation rather than starting from scratch.

Branding: Consistent styles reinforce brand recognition and help differentiate your brand from competitors.

Coherence: Design styles unify diverse elements, such as imagery, fonts, and colors, creating a seamless and coherent visual language.

Crafting Design Templates: A Step-by-Step Guide

Design templates serve as the backbone of your projects, providing a foundation that aligns with your brand's identity and values.

Identify Key Components: Determine the essential elements for your template, such as headers, body text, image placeholders, and call-to-action buttons.

Create Layouts: Design various layout options that cater to different materials and platforms. For instance, a social media template may have a different layout than a presentation template.

Incorporate Branding: Infuse the template with your brand's design styles, including typography, color palette, and imagery.

Customization Options: Design templates should be versatile enough to accommodate different types of content. Consider using placeholders and guides to make customization easier.

Developing Design Styles: The Art of Visual Consistency

Design styles are the threads that weave through your brand's visual identity. Defining and maintaining these styles is key to a consistent and impactful design presence.

Typography: Choose a set of fonts that reflect your brand's personality—typefaces for headings, subheadings, and body text that work cohesively together.

Color Palette: Establish a color palette that resonates with your brand's values and evokes the desired emotions. Use these colors consistently across all materials.

Imagery Guidelines: Define the types of images that align with your brand. This could involve specific filters, compositions, or themes.

Icons and Graphics: Develop a library of icons and graphics that encapsulate your brand's visual style. These can be used consistently to enhance your designs.

The Ripple Effect of Consistency

When templates and styles are utilized effectively, they extend their influence beyond individual projects, creating a ripple effect that enhances the overall brand experience.

Branding Coherence: Consistent templates and styles create a unified brand identity that's instantly recognizable across materials and platforms.

User Experience: A cohesive design language improves user experience, guiding users intuitively through your content.

Trust and Credibility: Consistency breeds trust and credibility. A consistent design aesthetic signals professionalism and attention to detail.

Flexibility and Scalability: Templates and styles provide a foundation that's adaptable to various contexts, ensuring that your brand remains consistent as it grows and evolves.

Conclusion

Creating templates and styles is an art that empowers designers to craft a harmonious and cohesive visual identity. By forging a foundation of design templates that cater to various materials and platforms, and by defining consistent design styles that encompass typography, color, imagery, and more, designers can ensure that their projects resonate with audiences, leaving a lasting impact. In the hands of skilled designers, templates and styles transform design into a symphony of consistency, guiding viewers through a captivating journey that speaks volumes about a brand's identity, values, and aspirations.

USING LIBRARIES AND SYMBOLS FOR REUSABLE DESIGN ELEMENTS

In the ever-evolving landscape of digital design, efficiency and consistency are prized virtues. The ability to create designs that are both visually captivating and time-effective is a goal shared by designers worldwide. Enter libraries and symbols—an indispensable duo that empowers designers to streamline workflows, enhance consistency, and infuse projects with a touch of magic. In this comprehensive article, we will delve into the world of libraries and symbols, exploring how these tools transform the design process by offering reusable elements that elevate both aesthetics and productivity.

Understanding Libraries and Symbols: Design's Dynamic Duo

Libraries: Design libraries are repositories that house a collection of reusable assets, including icons, images, graphics, and templates. These assets are organized for easy access and can be shared across projects.

Symbols: Symbols are design elements that are grouped together as a single unit, allowing for easy replication and consistent updates. Symbols ensure that changes made to one instance are automatically applied to all instances throughout the project.

Benefits of Libraries and Symbols:

Time Efficiency: Libraries and symbols eliminate the need to recreate design elements from scratch. This streamlines the design process and saves valuable time.

Consistency: By using consistent design elements from libraries and symbols, you maintain a cohesive visual language across all projects.

Easy Updates: Symbols enable quick updates. If changes are made to a symbol, those changes automatically cascade to all instances, ensuring uniformity.

Collaboration: Libraries facilitate collaboration by enabling teams to work with the same set of assets, promoting consistency and reducing confusion.

Crafting Design Libraries: A Step-by-Step Guide

Creating a well-organized design library is a strategic investment that pays off in terms of efficiency and visual coherence.

Categorize Assets: Organize assets into categories that reflect their purpose, such as icons, logos, images, and templates.

File Naming Conventions: Develop a clear file naming convention to ensure assets are easily searchable. Consistency in naming aids in efficient retrieval.

Formats and Resolutions: Store assets in different formats and resolutions to cater to various project requirements.

Metadata and Descriptions: Include metadata and descriptions for each asset, providing context and usage information for fellow designers.

Leveraging Design Symbols: The Art of Consistency

Symbols are the embodiment of design consistency. They allow you to create complex designs while ensuring every instance remains in perfect harmony.

Create a Master Symbol: Design the core element you want to use as a symbol. This could be a logo, button, or any other repeating element.

Convert to Symbol: Select the element and convert it into a symbol using your design software's symbol creation feature.

Editing Master Symbol: If you need to make changes, edit the master symbol. These changes will automatically be reflected in all instances.

Instance Variations: Use symbol instances to create variations of the original. You can adjust color, size, and other properties while maintaining the core design.

The Synergy of Libraries and Symbols: A Design Revolution

The marriage of libraries and symbols creates a design ecosystem that's both efficient and aesthetically pleasing.

Efficient Workflows: Libraries streamline workflows, allowing designers to access assets with a few clicks rather than recreating them.

Consistent Branding: Symbols ensure consistent branding elements across all materials, maintaining brand integrity.

Responsive Design: Libraries and symbols are invaluable for responsive design, enabling elements to adapt to different screen sizes seamlessly.

Creative Freedom: By saving time on repetitive tasks, designers can allocate more time for creative exploration and innovation.

Conclusion

In the realm of digital design, libraries and symbols are the unsung heroes that empower designers to craft consistent and compelling creations. By thoughtfully organizing assets in libraries and harnessing the power of symbols to maintain consistency and efficiency, designers elevate their work to new heights. In this dynamic interplay of design elements, designers transcend the limitations of time-consuming tasks and forge a path toward artistic expression, innovation, and impactful design. In the hands of skilled designers, libraries and symbols aren't just tools; they're the keystones that unlock a realm of creative possibilities, resulting in designs that capture attention, resonate with audiences, and leave an indelible mark on the digital landscape.

AUTOMATING TASKS WITH SCRIPTS AND MACROS

In the realm of design, creativity knows no bounds, but time is often a precious resource. The convergence of artistry and efficiency is where automation shines. With the advent of scripts and macros, designers can harness the power of automation to streamline repetitive tasks, boost productivity, and unlock newfound creative potential. In this comprehensive article, we'll explore the art of automating tasks with scripts and macros, uncovering how designers leverage these tools to revolutionize workflows and create designs that captivate and inspire.

Understanding Scripts and Macros: The Architects of Efficiency

Scripts: Design scripts are sequences of commands that automate specific tasks or processes in design software. They can be written in programming languages like JavaScript, Python, or specific scripting languages provided by design tools.

Macros: Macros are recorded sequences of actions performed within a design software. These recorded actions can be replayed at any time, automating the steps required to accomplish a task.

Benefits of Automation:

Time Efficiency: Automation eliminates the need to perform repetitive tasks manually, freeing up valuable time for more creative endeavors.

Consistency: Automated processes ensure consistent results, reducing the risk of errors that can arise from manual tasks.

Enhanced Productivity: Designers can accomplish tasks more quickly and efficiently, leading to increased productivity and output.

Innovation: With more time on their hands, designers can focus on exploring new creative ideas and pushing the boundaries of design.

Creating and Implementing Scripts: A Step-by-Step Guide

Design scripts are versatile tools that can be tailored to address specific needs. Here's how designers can create and implement scripts effectively:

Identify Repetitive Tasks: Identify tasks that are performed frequently, such as resizing images, applying filters, or formatting text.

Choose a Scripting Language: Select a scripting language that's compatible with your design software. Popular choices include JavaScript and Python.

Write the Script: Write the script code that encapsulates the steps required to complete the task. This may involve interacting with the design software's API (Application Programming Interface).

Test and Refine: Test the script on sample projects to ensure it produces the desired results. Refine the script if necessary to address any issues.

Harnessing Macros for Efficient Workflows

Macros are a powerful tool for automating tasks within your design software. Here's how to create and utilize macros effectively:

Recording the Macro: Start recording a macro and perform the series of actions you want to automate. This could include applying filters, rearranging layers, or formatting text.

Stop Recording: Once the sequence is complete, stop recording the macro. Give it a descriptive name that reflects its purpose.

Playback and Customization: When you want to perform the same task again, simply play back the recorded macro. Some software allows you to customize playback speed and make adjustments.

The Art of Creative Automation

Automation isn't limited to mundane tasks; it can enhance the creative process itself.

Batch Processing: Automate the processing of multiple files simultaneously. This is especially useful for resizing images, converting file formats, and applying consistent filters.

Template Generation: Use scripts to generate templates with dynamic content placeholders, allowing for efficient customization.

Data Visualization: Automate the creation of charts, graphs, and infographics using data-driven design scripts.

Interactive Design: Scripts can enable the creation of interactive elements, enhancing user experiences in web and app design.

Unleashing Creative Potential Through Efficiency

The true beauty of automation lies in its ability to liberate designers from the constraints of repetitive tasks, allowing them to channel their creative energy into innovation and artistic expression.

Efficiency as a Canvas: Automation becomes the canvas on which designers paint their visions with speed and precision.

Experimentation and Iteration: With automation handling repetitive tasks, designers can focus on experimenting with new techniques and iterating on design concepts.

Efficiency in Collaboration: Automation enhances collaboration by ensuring consistency across designs, even when multiple designers are involved.

Enhanced Problem Solving: The time saved through automation can be invested in tackling complex design challenges and pushing boundaries.

Conclusion

The fusion of creativity and automation transforms design workflows into a symphony of efficiency and innovation. By embracing scripts and macros to automate tasks, designers elevate their work beyond the mundane and unlock time for creative exploration. These tools are not just shortcuts; they are the conduits through which designers amplify their artistic visions, producing designs that not only capture attention but also reflect the depth of their creative ingenuity. As designers embrace automation, they step into a realm where efficiency and innovation dance hand in hand, weaving a tapestry of designs that captivate, inspire, and transcend the limits of time.

Chapter 9: Advanced Tips for Illustration and Logo Design

COMBINING SHAPES AND EFFECTS FOR PROFESSIONAL LOGO CREATION

A logo is more than just a visual mark; it's the embodiment of a brand's identity and values. The process of logo creation demands a delicate balance between creativity, aesthetics, and a deep understanding of the brand's essence. Among the myriad tools and techniques at a designer's disposal, the art of combining shapes and effects stands as a cornerstone of professional logo design. In this comprehensive article, we will delve into the intricate world of logo creation, exploring how designers skillfully combine shapes and effects to craft logos that resonate, captivate, and leave an indelible mark on the world.

Understanding Logo Design: A Blend of Art and Strategy

Shapes: Shapes are the building blocks of logo design. Each shape evokes specific emotions and communicates subtle messages that align with the brand's identity.
Effects: Effects encompass a range of visual enhancements, including shadows, gradients, textures, and more. These effects add depth, dimension, and sophistication to logo designs.

The Power of Shapes in Logo Design:

Geometric Shapes: Geometric shapes convey stability, balance, and order. Circles evoke unity and wholeness, while squares and triangles imply strength and structure.

Organic Shapes: Organic shapes evoke feelings of naturalness, freedom, and creativity. These shapes often mirror elements found in the natural world.

Abstract Shapes: Abstract shapes offer versatility, allowing designers to convey complex ideas or emotions without being overly literal.

Leveraging Effects for Visual Impact:

Shadows and Depth: Adding subtle shadows and depth effects to logo elements creates a sense of realism and dimensionality.

Gradients: Gradients are a versatile tool for creating visual interest. They can add depth, highlight, and even create a sense of movement.

Textures and Patterns: Incorporating textures or patterns into logo elements can imbue them with a tactile quality, adding character and depth.

The Art of Combining Shapes and Effects: Steps to Success

Step 1: Conceptualization and Brand Understanding:

Client Brief: Understand the brand's values, target audience, and desired message. The logo should encapsulate these elements.

Concept Development: Brainstorm concepts that align with the brand's identity. Consider the shapes that best convey the desired emotions and attributes.

Step 2: Shape Selection and Composition:

Shape Psychology: Choose shapes that resonate with the brand's personality. Consider how geometric, organic, or abstract shapes align with the brand's essence.

Balanced Composition: Combine shapes in a way that creates a harmonious composition. Balance, symmetry, and negative space play pivotal roles in composition.

Step 3: Applying Visual Effects:

Shadow and Depth Effects: Apply subtle shadows to give shapes a sense of dimension, grounding them within the design.

Gradients for Depth: Use gradients to add depth and visual interest to logo elements. Experiment with different gradient directions and color combinations.

Textures and Patterns: Apply textures or patterns to certain shapes to add tactile depth and convey specific qualities, such as ruggedness or elegance.

Step 4: Iteration and Refinement:

Feedback Loop: Share the initial design with stakeholders or peers to gather feedback. Make necessary adjustments based on the feedback.

Simplicity and Clarity: While combining shapes and effects, ensure that the logo remains simple and clear. Avoid visual clutter that can dilute its impact.

The Fusion of Artistry and Strategy

The true magic of combining shapes and effects in logo design lies in the seamless blend of artistry and strategic intent.

Symbolism and Storytelling: Every shape and effect contributes to the logo's narrative. The combination tells a story that resonates with the audience.

Brand Identity: The fusion of shapes and effects creates a logo that is not just visually appealing, but also serves as a visual representation of the brand's identity.

Memorability and Versatility: A well-crafted logo, born from the fusion of shapes and effects, is memorable and versatile—able to adapt to different contexts while retaining its impact.

Conclusion

The process of logo creation is a dynamic dance between shapes and effects. As designers expertly combine geometric, organic, and abstract shapes with shadows, gradients, and textures, they craft logos that transcend mere visuals and become vessels of meaning and emotion. In this fusion of artistry and strategy, designers shape the essence of brands, capturing their core values and aspirations in a single mark. By mastering the interplay of shapes and effects, designers wield the power to create logos that captivate, inspire, and endure as timeless symbols of identity in a rapidly evolving world.

STRATEGIES FOR SIMPLIFYING COMPLEX IDEAS INTO MEMORABLE LOGOS

In the intricate realm of logo design, the art lies not only in crafting a visually appealing mark but also in distilling complex ideas into a single, unforgettable symbol. A logo is the face of a brand, and its impact hinges on the ability to communicate depth and nuance through simplicity. In this comprehensive article, we will delve into the world of logo design, uncovering strategies that adept designers employ to transform intricate concepts into logos that resonate, captivate, and etch themselves into the collective memory.

The Challenge of Complexity: Taming the Elements

Complex ideas are often rich in meaning, but translating them into a simplified logo requires a delicate touch. Here's how designers rise to the challenge:

Identify Core Concepts: Delve into the heart of the idea. Identify the key elements or values that define it.

Hierarchy of Importance: Determine which elements are most crucial to communicate. Prioritize these for inclusion in the logo.

Visual Metaphors: Utilize metaphors or symbols that represent the essence of the concept. These provide an immediate connection for viewers.

Strategies for Simplification: The Path to Memorable Design

Minimalism: Embrace the principle of "less is more." Strip away unnecessary elements, focusing on the essentials that convey the idea.

Negative Space: Harness negative space to create dual meanings or hidden symbols within the logo. This adds depth without visual clutter.

Abstraction: Translate complex ideas into abstract forms. These forms evoke curiosity, inviting viewers to interpret the logo's meaning.

Streamlining Elements: Simplify intricate shapes or patterns while retaining their essence. Reduce details without compromising recognition.

Creating an Unforgettable Visual Language: Step-by-Step Guide

Step 1: Conceptual Exploration:

Brand Understanding: Immerse yourself in the brand's identity, values, and goals. Grasp the essence of the complex idea to be distilled.

Research and Inspiration: Gather inspiration from various sources, exploring visual representations of related concepts.

Step 2: Core Element Identification:

Essential Elements: Identify the most vital aspects of the complex idea that must be communicated through the logo.

Visual Hierarchy: Determine which elements take precedence. This hierarchy guides the design process.

Step 3: Symbolic Language Creation:

Metaphors and Symbols: Brainstorm metaphors or symbols that encapsulate the core idea. These serve as the foundation of the logo's visual language.

Simplification and Abstraction: Begin simplifying the chosen metaphors or symbols. Experiment with abstraction to distill the essence further.

Step 4: Iteration and Refinement:

Multiple Concepts: Develop multiple logo concepts based on the simplified metaphors. Each concept represents a different angle of the complex idea.

Feedback and Adaptation: Share the concepts with stakeholders for feedback. Adapt and refine the chosen concept based on feedback.

Crafting Complexity in Simplicity

The true artistry of logo design lies in crafting a symbol that is simultaneously simple yet profound.

Memorable Impact: The beauty of simplicity is its lasting impact. A simple logo is easier for the mind to remember and recall.

Universal Understanding: Simplicity transcends language and culture. A well-designed logo communicates universally.

Visual Elegance: A simplified logo possesses a visual elegance that captivates viewers. The absence of clutter allows the eye to focus on the core message.

The Elegance of Understatement: The Ultimate Goal

In the journey from complexity to simplicity, designers create logos that speak volumes through their understated elegance.

Essence Captured: An elegantly simple logo captures the essence of the complex idea without overwhelming the viewer.

Meaningful Connection: A simple logo connects emotionally with the audience, resonating on a deeper level.

Enduring Legacy: An elegant logo stands the test of time, retaining its impact and relevance even as trends evolve.

Conclusion

Creating a memorable logo from a complex idea is a true art—a dance between depth and simplicity. As designers navigate the delicate balance between abstraction and symbolism, they forge logos that become more than just visual marks; they become vessels of meaning, emotion, and identity. Through the strategic selection of core elements, the skillful application of minimalist principles, and the crafting of an elegant visual language, designers create logos that transcend the complexities of the original idea. These logos are not just symbols; they are gateways to profound concepts, etching themselves into the minds and hearts of viewers, and standing as a testament to the power of design to simplify, amplify, and inspire.

Chapter 10: Pushing the Boundaries: 3D Design and Perspective

EXPLORING COREL DRAW'S 3D TOOLS AND CAPABILITIES

In the realm of design, the allure of three-dimensionality is undeniable. The ability to transform flat surfaces into dynamic, immersive forms breathes life into creations, captivating audiences and elevating visual experiences. CorelDRAW, a stalwart in the design software landscape, empowers designers to venture into this captivating dimension with its array of 3D tools and capabilities. In this comprehensive article, we embark on a journey into CorelDRAW's 3D realm, unveiling the tools, techniques, and creative possibilities that await designers seeking to infuse their projects with depth, realism, and impact.

Understanding CorelDRAW's 3D Capabilities: A Multidimensional Toolkit

Extrude: Extrude takes 2D objects and transforms them into 3D forms by adding depth and volume. This tool gives a tangible feel to designs, making them pop off the canvas.

Bevel: The Bevel tool creates 3D effects by adding depth and contour to edges, simulating light and shadow interaction for a realistic appearance.

3D Effects: CorelDRAW offers a range of 3D effects, including Perspective, Revolve, and Rotate, enabling designers to craft intricate 3D shapes and designs.

3D Rotation: This tool empowers designers to rotate objects freely in three dimensions, adding a sense of dynamism and exploration to their designs.

Exploring CorelDRAW's 3D World: A Creative Odyssey

Step 1: Design Ideation and Conceptualization:

Concept Clarity: Understand the idea you want to transform into a 3D design. This could be a logo, an illustration, or any other design element.

Storyboarding: Sketch out the design from different angles to visualize how the 3D effect will enhance its impact.

Step 2: Applying 3D Effects:

Extrusion Magic: Use the Extrude tool to give flat shapes a newfound depth. Imagine turning a logo into a sculptural masterpiece.

Bevel Elegance: Apply the Bevel tool to edges, creating highlights and shadows that mimic real-world lighting, adding a touch of realism.

Step 3: Layering and Composition:

Depth Hierarchy: Organize the layers in your design to reflect depth and order, enhancing the sense of dimensionality.

Light and Shadow Interaction: Manipulate shadows to interact naturally with your 3D elements, amplifying the sense of realism.

Step 4: Texturing and Material Realism:

Textures for Authenticity: Apply textures to your 3D objects, simulating materials like metal, wood, or fabric for heightened realism.

Reflection and Refraction: Use the interactive tools to control reflection and refraction, mimicking how light interacts with different surfaces.

Step 5: Iteration and Refinement:

Visualization: Experiment with different angles, lighting setups, and textures to visualize how your 3D design will look from various perspectives.

Feedback Loop: Share your work with peers or clients to gather feedback and make necessary adjustments for a polished result.

The Creative Potential of CorelDRAW's 3D Tools:

Bringing Designs to Life: CorelDRAW's 3D tools breathe life into static designs, infusing them with depth, texture, and realism.

Visual Storytelling: 3D elements enrich the narrative of your designs, conveying messages and emotions with greater impact.

Product Design and Prototyping: Designers can create 3D mockups of products, enabling visualization and prototyping before production.

Harnessing 3D Tools for Innovation and Impact:

Product Packaging: Design captivating product packaging with 3D elements that showcase products from all angles.

Logo Evolution: Transform flat logos into multidimensional brand identities that stand out in a competitive landscape.

Architectural Visualization: CorelDRAW's 3D tools facilitate the creation of architectural mockups and visualizations.

Conclusion

In the realm of design, dimensionality isn't merely a visual luxury; it's a powerful tool that shapes how audiences perceive and engage with creations. CorelDRAW's 3D tools and capabilities unlock a world of possibilities, enabling designers to transcend flat surfaces and delve into the realm of depth, texture, and realism. By skillfully navigating the Extrude, Bevel, and other 3D tools, designers transform designs into interactive experiences that captivate, resonate, and inspire. As designers embrace CorelDRAW's 3D capabilities, they embark on a journey of innovation, breathing life into ideas and defying the constraints of two-dimensionality. This journey is an exploration of creativity, pushing the boundaries of design to unveil a world where imagination is the only limit and depth is the key to unlocking impactful visual narratives.

DESIGNING 3D OBJECTS WITH DEPTH, SHADING, AND PERSPECTIVE

In the realm of design, the quest for visual impact is a perpetual journey. Among the many techniques that empower designers to create compelling visuals, the art of designing 3D objects with depth, shading, and perspective stands as a cornerstone of artistic prowess. By infusing two-dimensional canvases with the illusion of three-dimensionality, designers can captivate audiences, evoke emotions, and breathe life into their creations. In this comprehensive article, we embark on an exploration of the techniques and strategies that underlie the creation of 3D objects with depth, shading, and perspective, unveiling the multidimensional world that exists beyond the surface.

Understanding the Magic of 3D Design: A Triad of Techniques

Depth: Depth is the foundation of three-dimensionality. It's the concept of objects receding into space, creating a sense of distance and proportion within a composition.

Shading: Shading involves the use of light and shadow to create the illusion of form and volume. It adds depth and realism to objects by mimicking the way light interacts with surfaces.

Perspective: Perspective is the visual representation of how objects appear smaller as they recede into the distance. It's a key technique for creating the illusion of depth and spatial relationships.

Crafting 3D Objects: The Creative Odyssey

Step 1: Conceptualization and Planning:

Idea Clarity: Understand the object you want to design in 3D. Visualize how it will appear from different angles.

Spatial Composition: Sketch out the composition, determining where the object will be placed in relation to other elements.

Step 2: Creating Depth:

Layering: Organize your design elements into layers that reflect their distance from the viewer. Foreground elements should overlap background elements.

Size Variation: Objects that are closer to the viewer should be larger, while objects in the distance should be smaller, adhering to the principles of perspective.

Step 3: Applying Shading:

Light Source Placement: Determine the direction of the light source. Consistency in light source placement is crucial for realistic shading.

Highlights and Shadows: Use highlights to indicate areas directly hit by light and shadows to show areas in the object's shade.

Step 4: Mastering Perspective:

Linear Perspective: Use linear perspective techniques to create the illusion of distance and depth. Vanishing points guide the placement of objects.

Foreshortening: Foreshortening involves depicting objects in a way that reflects their true proportions despite their skewed appearance due to perspective.

Step 5: Texture and Detailing:

Texture Mapping: Apply textures to your 3D object to enhance realism. Use shading to emphasize texture details.

Depth in Detail: Incorporate depth within textures to make the object's surface appear realistic, accounting for variations in lighting.

The Symphony of Dimensionality: Strategies for Impactful Design

Visual Hierarchy: Leverage depth, shading, and perspective to establish a clear visual hierarchy in your composition, guiding the viewer's gaze.

Emotional Impact: By creating depth and using shading to evoke realism, designers can imbue their designs with emotional resonance.

Dynamic Composition: Incorporating perspective into compositions adds dynamism, creating a sense of movement and engagement for the viewer.

Harnessing 3D Techniques for Various Contexts:

Product Design: Realistic 3D renderings of products provide clients with a tangible preview before manufacturing.

Architectural Visualization: Perspective and shading are essential in creating architectural renderings that accurately portray spatial relationships.

Illustration and Animation: Depth, shading, and perspective bring illustrations and animations to life, creating immersive experiences.

Conclusion

The art of designing 3D objects with depth, shading, and perspective is a symphony of techniques that transcend flat surfaces and transport viewers into multidimensional worlds. By mastering these techniques, designers wield the power to manipulate spatial relationships, evoke emotions, and tell visual stories that captivate and resonate. In the fusion of depth and shading, artists create the illusion of touchable forms, while the application of perspective adds a dynamic dimension of realism and movement. As designers explore the possibilities of these techniques, they open the gateway to a realm where canvas becomes cosmos, surfaces become sculptures, and visuals become visceral experiences. In this dynamic interplay of depth, shading, and perspective, designers rise beyond the realm of two-dimensionality, unveiling designs that transcend the ordinary and ignite the imagination.

INTEGRATING 3D ELEMENTS INTO 2D DESIGNS SEAMLESSLY

The intersection of two dimensions and three dimensions is a realm of creative possibility that holds tremendous allure for designers. Merging the tactile realism of 3D elements with the artistic allure of 2D designs gives birth to compositions that captivate, intrigue, and push the boundaries of visual storytelling. In this comprehensive article, we embark on a journey into the art of seamlessly integrating 3D elements into 2D designs, exploring the techniques, challenges, and boundless creative potential that lie within this dynamic fusion.

Understanding the Fusion of 2D and 3D: A Harmonious Coexistence

2D Elements: These are the traditional, flat design components that occupy the realm of width and height without the depth of 3D space.

3D Elements: These are objects or elements that occupy space with width, height, and depth, lending a sense of realism and tangibility to the design.

The Magic of Integration: Techniques and Strategies

Compositional Unity: 2D and 3D elements must coexist harmoniously within a composition. Unity in color, style, and perspective ensures a seamless blend.

Depth and Layering: Layer 3D elements strategically within the 2D design to create a sense of depth and perspective, enhancing realism.

Lighting Consistency: Ensure the lighting conditions of the 2D and 3D elements match to maintain the illusion of a shared environment.

Shadow Play: Accurate depiction of shadows cast by 3D elements is crucial for their integration into the 2D design.

Reflection Realism: Reflections on 3D elements should adhere to the reflective qualities of the 2D environment.

Seamless Texturing: Apply textures to 3D elements that match the design's overall aesthetic, allowing them to seamlessly blend with 2D elements.

Layer Management: Organize layers meticulously to separate 2D and 3D components while maintaining a coherent visual hierarchy.

Depth Cues and Perspective: Utilize techniques such as linear perspective and overlapping to visually anchor 3D elements within the 2D space.

Creating a Harmonious Fusion: A Step-by-Step Guide

Step 1: Conceptual Framework:

Design Purpose: Understand why you're integrating 3D elements. Define how they enhance the narrative or visual impact of the 2D design.

Story Mapping: Chart a visual story that outlines the interaction between 2D and 3D elements. Decide where each element comes into play.

Step 2: 2D Design Foundation:

Initial Design: Develop the 2D design as the canvas upon which 3D elements will be layered. Establish color palettes, visual style, and composition.

Layer Organization: Set up layers that categorize different design elements. This foundation ensures a structured integration process.

Step 3: Integration of 3D Elements:

Modeling and Texturing: Create or import 3D models that match the overall design aesthetic. Apply textures that align with the 2D environment.

Placement and Scale: Position 3D elements within the 2D composition. Scale them to fit seamlessly while adhering to perspective rules.

Lighting and Shadows: Match lighting conditions and cast realistic shadows to anchor 3D elements within the 2D space.

Step 4: Refinement and Review:

Realism Assessment: Analyze the design for visual coherence. Check that shadows, reflections, and lighting align naturally.

Feedback Loop: Share the integrated design with peers or clients for feedback. Make necessary adjustments to achieve a flawless blend.

The Synergy of Two Realms: Crafting a Masterpiece

Immersive Storytelling: Integration adds a layer of depth that amplifies the narrative impact of the design, drawing viewers into a multisensory experience.
Visually Arresting: The interplay of 2D and 3D elements creates visuals that command attention, arousing curiosity and exploration.

Expanding Creative Horizons: Merging dimensions opens a gateway to a universe where imagination knows no bounds. Designs become limitless tapestries.

Design Applications and Beyond: A World of Creative Exploration

Advertising Campaigns: Integrated 2D and 3D designs infuse advertising visuals with depth, enhancing brand impact and message delivery.

Web Design: Seamless integration transforms web interfaces, offering interactive experiences that leave lasting impressions.

Editorial Illustrations: Magazines and books can leverage 3D integration to add an interactive layer to their printed content.

Conclusion

The integration of 3D elements into 2D designs is a testament to the malleability of creativity. Designers who venture into this multidimensional realm wield the power to craft compositions that transcend conventional boundaries. As they master techniques that bridge the gap between dimensions, designers orchestrate visual symphonies that resonate with audiences on emotional, aesthetic, and intellectual levels. In the seamless fusion of 2D and 3D, artists create designs that transcend the ordinary, forging connections between realms that captivate, provoke thought, and redefine the parameters of visual expression. In this realm of creative synergy, the canvas transforms into a cosmos, breathing life into design and design into an immersive experience that lingers in the minds and hearts of all who behold it.

Chapter 11: Creative Tips for UI/UX Design and Web Graphics

DESIGNING USER INTERFACES WITH PRECISION AND AESTHETICS

In the digital age, where interactions happen at the swipe of a finger and the click of a mouse, user interfaces (UI) play a pivotal role in shaping user experiences. A well-designed UI is more than just a visual arrangement of elements; it's a harmonious symphony of precision and aesthetics that guides users through digital landscapes effortlessly. In this comprehensive article, we embark on a journey into the realm of UI design, unraveling the techniques, principles, and creative nuances that underpin the creation of interfaces that captivate, engage, and elevate user interactions.

Understanding UI Design: A Fusion of Form and Function

User-Centered Design: UI design revolves around the needs and behaviors of users. It's about creating interfaces that are intuitive, efficient, and enjoyable to use.

Visual Hierarchy: Aesthetic organization of elements guides users' attention, emphasizing what's important and leading them through the interface.

Color and Typography: Color choices and typography contribute to the interface's personality, evoke emotions, and enhance readability.

The Marriage of Precision and Aesthetics: Techniques and Strategies

Wireframing and Prototyping: Begin with wireframes that outline the interface's layout and structure. Prototypes bring wireframes to life, showcasing interactions.

Responsive Design: Create interfaces that adapt seamlessly to various screen sizes and devices, ensuring a consistent experience for users.

Consistency and Pattern Libraries: Establish design patterns for elements like buttons, forms, and navigation, ensuring a cohesive and recognizable interface.

Microinteractions: Design small, subtle animations and interactions that provide feedback, guide users, and add a layer of delight.

Accessibility: Design interfaces that are inclusive, considering users with disabilities. Ensure proper contrast, readable fonts, and keyboard navigation.
Designing for Touch: When designing for touch devices, consider touch-friendly elements, spacing, and gestures that enhance the tactile experience.

The UI Design Journey: Crafting a User-Centric Experience

Step 1: User Research and Analysis:

User Persona Creation: Understand your target users' demographics, behaviors, and needs to inform your design decisions.

Competitor Analysis: Study similar interfaces to identify strengths, weaknesses, and opportunities for differentiation.

Step 2: Information Architecture:

Content Hierarchy: Organize content in a logical hierarchy, ensuring that users find what they need effortlessly.

Navigation Design: Design intuitive navigation menus and structures that guide users through the interface seamlessly.

Step 3: Visual Design:

Color Palette and Typography: Choose colors that resonate with your brand and typography that ensures readability across different devices.

Iconography: Design icons that are universally recognizable and align with the interface's overall aesthetic.

Step 4: Prototyping and Testing:

Interactive Prototypes: Create interactive prototypes that allow users to experience how the interface will function.

Usability Testing: Conduct usability testing to gather feedback and identify areas for improvement.

Step 5: Iteration and Refinement:

Feedback Incorporation: Based on user feedback, refine the design, interactions, and any usability issues.

Fine-Tuning: Pay attention to minute details like spacing, alignment, and microinteractions to ensure a polished interface.

Achieving the Perfect Blend: Aesthetic Precision and Functional Elegance

Enhanced Usability: A well-designed UI simplifies user interactions, reducing frustration and enhancing user satisfaction.

Engaging Experiences: Aesthetic elements and thoughtful interactions create engaging experiences that keep users coming back.

Brand Consistency: A well-designed UI reflects your brand's identity, fostering a sense of trust and familiarity.

Design Applications and Beyond: Exploring UI in Various Contexts

Mobile Apps: UI design is crucial for mobile apps, where space is limited, and ease of use is paramount. Web Design: Web interfaces need to balance aesthetics with efficient navigation to engage users across various pages.
Software Interfaces: Software UI must be intuitive, streamlining complex processes for users.

Conclusion

In the ever-evolving digital landscape, UI design is the bridge between users and technology. It's the fusion of aesthetics and functionality that transforms digital interactions into memorable experiences. By mastering the techniques of wireframing, responsive design, microinteractions, and more, designers create interfaces that seamlessly guide users through their digital journeys. In the harmonious blend of precision and aesthetics, the UI becomes more than a tool—it's a storyteller, an enabler, and a vessel for creativity. As designers breathe life into pixels, they sculpt experiences that delight, inspire, and leave lasting impressions in the minds of users. In the realm of UI design, precision and aesthetics come together to shape the future of digital experiences, where each tap, swipe, and click unfolds a story of user-centric creativity.

OPTIMIZING WEB GRAPHICS FOR FAST LOADING AND RESPONSIVENESS

In the age of lightning-fast internet connections and mobile browsing dominance, the performance of a website is paramount. Central to this performance is the optimization of web graphics, a practice that bridges the gap between visual allure and seamless user experiences. The pursuit of swift loading times and responsiveness demands a meticulous understanding of formats, compression techniques, and adaptive designs. In this comprehensive article, we delve into the realm of web graphic optimization, uncovering the strategies, tools, and creative methods that ensure your website's visual assets shine without compromising speed and user satisfaction.

Understanding Web Graphic Optimization: Where Form Meets Function

Fast Loading: Swift loading times are critical for retaining visitors. Studies have shown that users abandon websites that take more than a few seconds to load.

Responsiveness: In the era of various devices and screen sizes, responsive design ensures that web graphics adapt seamlessly to different contexts.

Visual Quality: Balancing optimization and visual quality is an art. Strive for crisp, clear graphics that maintain their allure despite compression.

Strategies for Swift Loading and Responsiveness: A Digital Arsenal

Image Formats: Different image formats serve varying purposes. JPEG for photographs, PNG for transparent images, and SVG for vector graphics.

Compression Techniques: Employ lossless or lossy compression to reduce image file sizes without compromising visual quality significantly.

Retina Graphics: Provide high-resolution graphics for devices with retina displays, ensuring pixel-perfect clarity.

Lazy Loading: Load images only when they come into the user's view, preventing unnecessary data usage and speeding up initial page load times.

Adaptive Images: Serve different image sizes based on the user's device, screen size, and resolution.

Optimization for Different Formats: A Deep Dive

JPEG Optimization:

Quality Settings: Adjust JPEG quality settings to balance compression and image clarity.

Progressive JPEGs: Use progressive JPEGs that load in multiple passes, allowing for faster rendering of lower-quality versions.

PNG Optimization:

Selective Use: Opt for PNGs when transparency is required. For simpler images, consider converting them to JPEG.

PNG-8 vs. PNG-24: Use PNG-8 for images with a limited color palette and PNG-24 for images with a wide range of colors.

SVG Optimization:

Minification: Minify SVG code by removing unnecessary tags, spaces, and comments.

Responsive SVG: Design SVG graphics to be responsive, adjusting their size and proportions to fit various screen sizes.

Tools for Seamless Optimization: Navigating the Toolkit

Image Editors: Popular tools like Adobe Photoshop, Adobe Illustrator, and CorelDRAW provide optimization features.

Online Compression Tools: Platforms like TinyPNG, Compressor.io, and ImageOptim optimize images without compromising quality.

Content Delivery Networks (CDNs): CDNs distribute website content across multiple servers, reducing load times through caching and optimized routing.

Website Performance Plugins: Platforms like WordPress offer plugins that automatically optimize images upon upload.

The Optimization Journey: Crafting a Performance-Driven Experience

Step 1: Image Selection and Preparation:

Strategic Choices: Select the right image format based on the type of content. Compress images before uploading.

Image Dimensions: Resize images to their intended display size to prevent browsers from rendering unnecessary pixels.

Step 2: Compression and Quality Control:

Compression Tools: Use online tools or image editors to compress images while maintaining acceptable quality.

Quality Inspection: Review compressed images to ensure they maintain clarity and detail.

Step 3: Implementation and Testing:

Responsive Design: Implement responsive design techniques to ensure images adapt to various screen sizes.

Lazy Loading: Implement lazy loading for images to prioritize the loading of visible content.

Step 4: Monitoring and Iteration:

Performance Testing: Regularly test your website's performance using tools like Google PageSpeed Insights or GTmetrix.

Feedback and Refinement: Gather feedback from users and analyze performance data. Refine image optimization as needed.

Achieving Balance: A Harmonious Web Experience

User-Centric Performance: Swift loading and responsive graphics put user experience at the forefront, reducing bounce rates and increasing engagement.

Brand Integrity: Optimal graphics maintain brand aesthetics without sacrificing speed, ensuring a consistent user perception.

Search Engine Optimization (SEO): Search engines consider page loading times as a ranking factor, emphasizing the importance of optimization.

The Spectrum of Web Optimization: Adapting to Varying Contexts

E-Commerce: Swift loading times are critical for online stores, where delays can lead to abandoned carts.

Media-Rich Sites: Image-heavy websites must prioritize optimization to strike a balance between visuals and speed.

Portfolio Sites: Visual artists and photographers should showcase their work with high-quality images that load quickly.
Conclusion

The pursuit of optimal web graphics is a delicate dance between visual appeal and digital performance. In the realm of web design, every pixel counts, and every second matters.

CREATING INTERACTIVE ELEMENTS AND PROTOTYPES WITHIN COREL DRAW

The world of design has evolved from static visuals to dynamic, interactive experiences that engage and captivate users. In this modern landscape, creating interactive elements and prototypes is a vital skill for designers, as it bridges the gap between concept and reality. CorelDRAW, a versatile design tool, offers a host of features that enable designers to craft immersive interactions and functional prototypes that breathe life into their creations. In this comprehensive article, we delve into the realm of interactive design and prototyping within CorelDRAW, uncovering techniques, tools, and creative methods that empower designers to turn ideas into interactive realities.

Understanding Interactive Design and Prototyping: Where Creativity Meets Functionality

Interactivity: Interactive design involves creating elements that respond to user actions, enhancing user engagement and creating intuitive experiences.

Prototyping: Prototypes are mockups or simulations of a design, allowing designers and stakeholders to test and refine functionality before development.

Dynamic Elements and Prototypes: The CorelDRAW Arsenal

Object States: Utilize object states to create different versions of an object based on user interactions, such as hover effects or button states.

Hyperlinks: Transform static elements into clickable links that navigate users to different parts of the design or external websites.

Interactive PDFs: Convert your CorelDRAW designs into interactive PDFs that retain clickable links and other interactive elements.

Animation Tools: CorelDRAW's animation tools allow you to create simple animations for elements like buttons or illustrations.

Prototyping Techniques: Build functional prototypes that simulate user interactions, enabling testing and refinement of the user experience.

Step-by-Step Guide to Crafting Interactive Elements and Prototypes

Step 1: Conceptualization and Planning:

User Journey Mapping: Map out the user's journey through the interactive elements to identify touchpoints and interactions.

Defining Interactions: Determine the desired behavior of each interactive element—hover effects, clicks, transitions, etc.

Step 2: Designing Interactive Elements:

Creating Object States: Duplicate objects to represent different states (normal, hover, clicked) and apply changes to achieve interactivity.

Adding Hyperlinks: Use the Hyperlink tool to transform objects into clickable links. Define the destination URL or page.

Step 3: Animation and Prototyping:

Animating Objects: Utilize animation tools to add simple animations, like fades or movements, to interactive elements.

Prototyping Process: Create separate pages or artboards to simulate different screens or interactions within your design.

Step 4: Refinement and Testing:

Functional Testing: Test the interactivity and functionality of your elements and prototypes to ensure a seamless user experience.

User Feedback: Share your interactive design or prototype with users or stakeholders to gather feedback and make necessary improvements.

The Dynamics of Creativity and Functionality: Crafting User-Centric Experiences

Engaging User Experience: Interactive elements enrich user interactions, making designs more engaging, intuitive, and memorable.

User-Centered Design: Prototyping allows designers to gather insights and refine the user experience before development begins.

Functional Demonstrations: Prototypes provide stakeholders with a tangible understanding of the final product's functionality.

Applications and Beyond: Exploring Interactive Design in Various Contexts

Web Design: Interactive elements are fundamental for websites, enhancing navigation, engagement, and user satisfaction.

App Design: Prototypes simulate app interactions, aiding in refining functionality and user flow before development.

Presentation Materials: Interactive PDFs elevate presentations by allowing viewers to engage with content beyond static visuals.

Conclusion

In the dynamic world of design, the fusion of creativity and functionality reigns supreme. CorelDRAW, with its diverse toolkit, empowers designers to transform static designs into interactive experiences that captivate, engage, and inspire. By embracing object states, hyperlinks, animation, and prototyping, designers bring their visions to life, allowing users to interact with content in meaningful ways. Interactive design and prototyping within CorelDRAW not only enhance user experiences but also streamline design iterations, fostering collaboration and innovation. As designers navigate this realm of interactivity, they embark on a journey of creativity and functionality, where every click, hover, and transition unfolds a narrative of seamless, user-centered design.

Conclusion

REFLECTING ON THE JOURNEY FROM NOVICE TO PROFESSIONAL IN COREL DRAW

Every creative journey begins with a spark of curiosity and a desire to express oneself. For many, this journey evolves from stumbling steps to confident strides, leading to the realm of professionalism. CorelDRAW, a powerful graphic design software, has been the canvas upon which countless designers have painted their progress from novice to expert. In this reflective article, we delve into the transformative journey of transitioning from a novice to a professional in CorelDRAW, exploring the stages, challenges, growth, and milestones that shape this remarkable progression.

The Novice Stage: A Humble Beginning

Exploration: The journey commences with exploration. Novices navigate through menus, tools, and features, marveling at the possibilities.

Trial and Error: The initial stages involve experimentation—trying out tools, creating shapes, and getting a feel for the software's capabilities.

Frustration and Learning: Novices often encounter frustration as concepts like layers, nodes, and vector editing can be initially overwhelming. This stage is marked by an insatiable thirst for learning.

Challenges and Growth: The Path to Proficiency

Concept Grasping: With time, novices begin to understand core concepts like vector graphics, object manipulation, and basic design principles.

Skill Acquisition: Learning to use tools effectively and efficiently is key. Mastery of shortcuts, tools, and techniques becomes a priority.

Tackling Complexity: Novices transition from basic shapes to more complex designs, tackling challenges that demand attention to detail and creativity.

Mentorship and Learning Resources: Seeking guidance from tutorials, online communities, and mentors accelerates growth, offering insights and shortcuts.

Embracing Professionalism: The Transition

Confidence: As novices accumulate knowledge, their confidence grows. They are no longer intimidated by complex projects.

Creative Independence: Professionals venture beyond tutorials, using CorelDRAW as a blank canvas for their own creative visions.

Efficiency and Workflow: Professionals streamline their workflow, utilizing shortcuts, custom workspaces, and efficient layer management.

Attention to Detail: Mastery involves refining designs, paying meticulous attention to elements like typography, color theory, and composition.

Creating for Clients: Transitioning to a professional often involves working for clients, translating creative concepts into practical solutions.

Reflecting on the Journey: Milestones and Insights

Mastering Tools: The ability to leverage CorelDRAW's tools, from basic shapes to advanced effects, marks a significant milestone.

Understanding Layers and Object Management: Proficiency in layer management streamlines design and ensures a structured workflow.

Efficient Workflow: Professionals navigate CorelDRAW with finesse, using keyboard shortcuts and toolbars to create seamlessly.

Artistry and Style: The development of a personal style and artistic voice distinguishes a professional's work, making it recognizable and unique.

Client Success: Successfully delivering projects that meet clients' expectations and needs is a testament to professional growth.

Looking Ahead: Continuous Learning and Innovation

Staying Curious: Professionals understand that the creative journey is ongoing. Staying curious about new features and trends is vital.

Adapting to Change: CorelDRAW evolves, introducing new tools and functionalities. Professionals embrace change and adapt accordingly.

Pushing Boundaries: From advanced techniques to exploring new design genres, professionals consistently push their creative boundaries.

Conclusion

The journey from novice to professional in CorelDRAW is a testament to the power of dedication, curiosity, and the relentless pursuit of excellence. From fumbling beginnings to confident design prowess, every designer's journey is a unique narrative of growth, learning, and transformation. CorelDRAW serves as both a mentor and a canvas, guiding novices along a path of skill acquisition and nurturing professionals in their pursuit of innovative design. As designers reflect on their journey, they recognize that the destination is ever-evolving, and the true beauty lies in the progression itself—a progression that echoes the fusion of passion, technique, and artistic vision.

EMPHASIZING THE IMPORTANCE OF CONTINUOUS LEARNING AND EXPERIMENTATION

In the dynamic realm of creativity, stagnation is the enemy and innovation is the ally. The journey from novice to expert, amateur to professional, is paved with continuous learning and fearless experimentation. This path is not a destination but a perpetual quest, where the hunger for knowledge and the audacity to venture beyond comfort zones drive artists, designers, and creators to new horizons of brilliance. In this comprehensive article, we delve into the essence of continuous learning and experimentation, uncovering the transformative power they hold for personal growth, creative evolution, and professional excellence.

The Spirit of Curiosity: Nurturing a Lifelong Learning Mindset

Learning as an Evolution: Creativity is not static; it evolves. Continuous learning is the fuel that propels creative evolution, keeping ideas fresh and perspectives dynamic.

Staying Relevant: Industries evolve, and new tools and techniques emerge. Lifelong learning ensures that skills stay current and adaptable to changing landscapes.

Breaking Barriers: Learning allows creators to break free from creative limitations, exploring uncharted territories and embracing the unknown.

Knowledge Diversification: Learning across disciplines exposes creators to new perspectives, infusing fresh insights into their primary field.

Embracing Fearless Experimentation: The Art of Pushing Boundaries

Breaking Comfort Zones: Experimentation encourages creators to move beyond the familiar, challenging them to embrace discomfort for creative growth.

Innovation through Failure: Failures become stepping stones to innovation. Experimentation teaches creators to learn from mistakes and evolve their approaches.

Personal Style Refinement: Experimentation helps creators refine their artistic voice and define their unique style, setting them apart from the crowd.

Unearthing Hidden Potential: Experimentation often uncovers unexpected strengths and abilities, leading creators down paths they never imagined.

Continuous Learning and Experimentation: A Dynamic Duo

Mutual Reinforcement: Learning and experimentation are mutually reinforcing. Knowledge gained from learning fuels fresh ideas for experimentation.

Evolving Creativity: Experimentation turns theoretical knowledge into practical wisdom, elevating creativity from conceptual to tangible.

Professional Edge: In the modern creative landscape, where innovation reigns, those who embrace continuous learning and experimentation gain a competitive edge.

Nurturing the Journey: Strategies for Embracing Learning and Experimentation

Setting Learning Goals: Define clear objectives for your learning journey. What skills, techniques, or knowledge do you want to acquire?

Diverse Learning Sources: Seek learning from a variety of sources—online courses, books, workshops, mentors, and even peers.

Practice and Application: Apply what you learn through practical projects. Experiment with new techniques and concepts to deepen understanding.

Cultivating Curiosity: Ask questions, challenge assumptions, and explore the "why" and "how" behind techniques and concepts.

Time Management: Allocate dedicated time for learning and experimentation, treating them as essential components of your creative routine.

Embracing a Growth Mindset: The Key to Sustained Progress

Openness to Feedback: A growth mindset invites constructive criticism, viewing it as a pathway to improvement rather than a setback.

Resilience in the Face of Challenges: A growth mindset sees challenges as opportunities to learn and evolve, not as insurmountable obstacles.

Celebrating Small Wins: Acknowledge and celebrate your progress, recognizing that even incremental improvements contribute to the bigger picture.

Conclusion: A Journey Without Bounds

The journey of continuous learning and fearless experimentation is not confined to a specific realm, medium, or occupation. It's a universal path that extends beyond disciplines, age, and boundaries. Whether you're a painter, writer, designer, or musician, the pursuit of excellence demands an unquenchable thirst for knowledge and the audacity to explore uncharted territories. It's a journey that acknowledges that true mastery is a moving target—one that requires persistent dedication to staying at the forefront of one's craft. By embracing this path, creators nurture a dynamic, ever-evolving creative spirit, producing work that not only stands the test of time but shapes it as well.

ENCOURAGING READERS TO APPLY THE TIPS AND TRICKS TO THEIR OWN DESIGN PROJECTS

Embarking on a creative journey is more than a solitary pursuit—it's an opportunity to wield newfound knowledge, techniques, and inspiration. The tips and tricks you've acquired along the way are the keys to unlocking your potential and transforming your vision into reality. In this article, we delve into the invigorating process of applying the tips and tricks you've learned to your design projects, infusing them with innovation, depth, and a touch of your unique style. Let's explore how you can turn these insights into actionable steps that propel your creativity to new heights.

1. Knowledge Into Action: Translating Tips into Tangible Steps

The first step is bridging the gap between theory and practice. Each tip you've gathered holds potential waiting to be unleashed. Break down these insights into actionable steps that align with your project's goals and scope.

2. Strategy and Planning: Crafting a Blueprint for Brilliance

Before diving in, strategize. Outline the objectives, target audience, and desired outcomes of your project. Which tips resonate most with your project's essence? Build a roadmap that ensures every tip is utilized purposefully.

3. Tool Mastery: Harnessing Techniques and Tools

Are there specific tools or techniques tied to the tips you've gathered? Mastery lies in their application. Whether it's vector manipulation, typography finesse, or color theory, delve into these tools with confidence.

4. Integration with Workflow: Streamlining Implementation

To prevent disjointed efforts, seamlessly integrate these tips into your design workflow. If you're refining typography, integrate it from the outset rather than as an afterthought. This ensures a holistic design process.

5. Iteration and Refinement: A Dance of Progress

Iteration is your ally. Apply the tips and tricks, then revisit and refine. This iterative cycle hones your design, uncovering nuances and hidden potentials you may have missed initially.

6. Personal Touch: Infusing Your Unique Style

While tips enhance design, your style defines it. Apply the tips but remember that innovation often lies at the intersection of technique and personal flair. Infuse your signature style into every aspect.

7. Feedback and Collaboration: Inviting Constructive Insights

Share your work with peers, mentors, or online communities. Feedback refines your application of tips and exposes blind spots. Collaboration introduces fresh perspectives.

8. Embrace Mistakes: Learning through Trials

Mistakes aren't setbacks; they're lessons. Embrace experimentation and the potential for missteps. Some of your most valuable insights will emerge from these moments.

9. Continuous Learning: An Ever-Growing Palette

Remember that learning is a lifelong journey. Continuously seek new tips, techniques, and trends. Apply these fresh insights to your future projects, ensuring your growth remains dynamic.

10. Celebrate Progress: Nurturing Your Creative Spirit

With each project, celebrate not just the finished product, but the journey itself. Recognize how far you've come, the skills you've honed, and the possibilities that lie ahead.

Unlocking Your Creative Potential: A Journey of Transformation

Applying tips and tricks to your design projects isn't just a mechanical process—it's a journey of transformation. It's about infusing your projects with the wisdom you've acquired, creating a bridge between your creative aspirations and the canvas before you. Every brushstroke, every click, and every design element you bring to life is a testament to your dedication, your growth, and your relentless pursuit of excellence.

So, as you embark on your next design endeavor, remember the treasure trove of tips and tricks at your disposal. Approach your project with intention, curiosity, and a willingness to explore uncharted territories. In doing so, you'll weave together your unique style, the power of knowledge, and the thrill of experimentation. With every design project, you breathe life into creativity, leaving your mark on the world—a mark that's not just a culmination of tips, but a masterpiece in its own right.

Appendix: Keyboard Shortcuts and Quick References
A HANDY REFERENCE GUIDE TO ESSENTIAL KEYBOARD SHORTCUTS

In the world of modern design and productivity, time is of the essence. The keyboard shortcuts at your fingertips are the secret keys to unlocking unparalleled efficiency, allowing you to navigate complex software, execute tasks, and unleash your creativity with lightning speed. This comprehensive reference guide delves into the essential keyboard shortcuts that are essential for designers, content creators, and professionals alike. From design software to general productivity tools, let's explore the shortcuts that will transform your workflow from mundane to magnificent.

Why Keyboard Shortcuts Matter: A Shortcut to Success

Keyboard shortcuts are more than just a collection of key combinations—they're the magic wands of productivity. They offer several advantages that elevate your workflow:

Speed: Perform tasks in a fraction of the time it would take with mouse navigation.

Efficiency: Seamlessly switch between tools and actions without disrupting your flow.

Precision: Execute actions precisely, reducing the chances of errors.

Fluid Workflow: Navigate through software interfaces seamlessly, focusing on creativity rather than tool hunting.

Popular Keyboard Shortcuts: A Designer's Arsenal

Note: The following shortcuts are based on common software such as Adobe Creative Suite and Microsoft Office. Please check your software's documentation for specific shortcuts.

General Shortcuts:

Ctrl (Cmd) + C: Copy selected item.
Ctrl (Cmd) + V: Paste copied item.
Ctrl (Cmd) + Z: Undo previous action.
Ctrl (Cmd) + S: Save your work.
Ctrl (Cmd) + X: Cut selected item.
Ctrl (Cmd) + A: Select all items.
Ctrl (Cmd) + F: Find or search for a specific item.
Ctrl (Cmd) + P: Print the current document.

Design Software Shortcuts:

V: Select the Move tool.
A: Select the Direct Selection tool.
B: Select the Brush tool.
E: Select the Eraser tool.
T: Select the Text tool.
G: Select the Gradient tool.
Ctrl (Cmd) + G: Group selected objects.
Ctrl (Cmd) + Shift + G: Ungroup objects.

Adobe Photoshop:

Ctrl (Cmd) + T: Transform selected item.
Ctrl (Cmd) + J: Duplicate selected layer.
Ctrl (Cmd) + Alt + Z: Step backward through history.

Adobe Illustrator:

Ctrl (Cmd) + 2: Lock selected object(s).
Ctrl (Cmd) + 8: Hide selected object(s).
Ctrl (Cmd) + D: Duplicate the last action.

Microsoft Word:

Ctrl (Cmd) + B: Bold selected text.
Ctrl (Cmd) + I: Italicize selected text.
Ctrl (Cmd) + U: Underline selected text.
Ctrl (Cmd) + L: Align text to the left.
Ctrl (Cmd) + R: Align text to the right.

Excel:

Ctrl (Cmd) + C: Copy selected cells.
Ctrl (Cmd) + V: Paste copied cells.
Ctrl (Cmd) + X: Cut selected cells.
Ctrl (Cmd) + Shift + L: Apply or remove filters.

Bringing It All Together: Harnessing Keyboard Shortcuts for Success

As you embark on your journey of productivity and creativity, harness the power of keyboard shortcuts to your advantage. Start by familiarizing yourself with the shortcuts relevant to your software and tasks. Create a cheat sheet or sticky note to have them at hand until they become second nature.
Practice is key. Implement these shortcuts in your workflow, one at a time. Gradually, you'll notice your actions becoming more fluid and your tasks completed in record time.

Customization is your friend. Many software programs allow you to customize shortcuts to match your preferences. Take advantage of this feature to optimize your workflow further.

Remember, mastery takes time. Don't be discouraged if you don't remember all the shortcuts at once. Over time, your efficiency will skyrocket, leaving you with more time and energy to focus on what truly matters—your creative endeavors and professional achievements.

QUICK TIPS AND REFERENCES FOR FREQUENTLY USED TOOLS AND FUNCTIONS

In the realm of design, efficiency isn't just a luxury—it's a necessity. The ability to swiftly wield your design software's tools and functions can be the difference between an ordinary project and an extraordinary masterpiece. This comprehensive guide is a treasure trove of quick tips and references for the most frequently used tools and functions across various design software. Whether you're a graphic designer, illustrator, or content creator, these insights will empower you to navigate your creative domain with finesse, precision, and unmatched efficiency.

Essential Keyboard Shortcuts: The Foundation of Speed and Precision

Keyboard shortcuts are your express lane to efficiency. Memorizing these shortcuts can drastically reduce the time spent navigating menus. Here are a few to get you started:

Ctrl (Cmd) + C: Copy selected item.
Ctrl (Cmd) + V: Paste copied item.
Ctrl (Cmd) + Z: Undo previous action.
Ctrl (Cmd) + S: Save your work.
Ctrl (Cmd) + X: Cut selected item.

Ctrl (Cmd) + A: Select all items.
Ctrl (Cmd) + F: Find or search for a specific item.
Ctrl (Cmd) + P: Print the current document.
Common Tools and Functions: Unleashing Creativity with Finesse

Brush Tool:

Adjust the brush size by using the bracket keys [and].
Shift + Click: Draw straight lines between two points.
Alt (Option) + Click: Sample a color from the image for the brush.

Pen Tool:

Click to add anchor points, and click and drag to create curved segments.
Convert anchor points between smooth and corner points using Ctrl (Cmd) + Alt (Option).
Ctrl (Cmd) + Click on anchor points to adjust their handles.

Text Tool:

Double-click on a word to select it, and triple-click to select the whole paragraph.
Ctrl (Cmd) + B: Bold selected text.
Ctrl (Cmd) + I: Italicize selected text.

Selection Tools:
Hold down Spacebar while using a selection tool to temporarily activate the Hand tool for panning.

Layers and Groups:

Ctrl (Cmd) + G: Group selected objects.
Ctrl (Cmd) + Shift + G: Ungroup objects.
Ctrl (Cmd) + 2: Lock selected layer.

Transformations and Alignments:

Ctrl (Cmd) + T: Free Transform selected item.
Ctrl (Cmd) + Shift + T: Duplicate the last transformation action.
Ctrl (Cmd) + Shift + O: Fit selected artboard to the window.

Zoom and Navigation:

Ctrl (Cmd) + Spacebar: Zoom in.
Ctrl (Cmd) + Alt (Option) + Spacebar: Zoom out.
Ctrl (Cmd) + 0: Fit the artboard to the window.

Color Management:

Use the Eyedropper tool to sample colors from images or objects.
Utilize the Color Picker to create and adjust color swatches.

Saving Time with Shortcuts and Workflows

Create custom keyboard shortcuts for frequently used functions to further enhance your workflow.
Utilize software presets to quickly apply preferred settings to new projects.
Experiment with action scripts and macros to automate repetitive tasks.

Conclusion: Design Brilliance at Your Fingertips

Mastering frequently used tools and functions is the cornerstone of becoming a design virtuoso. By internalizing keyboard shortcuts, understanding tool nuances, and optimizing workflows, you're equipping yourself to tackle design challenges with confidence and creativity.

As you incorporate these quick tips and references into your practice, you'll discover a newfound sense of control over your creative domain. With efficiency as your guiding star, you'll navigate the complexities of design software with the prowess of a seasoned professional, creating stunning visuals that leave a lasting impact. So, let your creativity flourish and your efficiency soar—because in the world of design, every second saved is a second invested in crafting remarkable works of art.

Glossary

DEFINITIONS OF KEY TERMS AND CONCEPTS USED THROUGHOUT THE BOOK

In the ever-evolving world of design, a lexicon of specialized terminology and concepts has emerged to describe the intricacies of the creative process. From vector manipulation to color theory, understanding these key terms is essential for anyone navigating the design landscape. This comprehensive guide serves as a reference, offering clear definitions of the most crucial terms and concepts used throughout the eBook. Whether you're a novice seeking to expand your design vocabulary or a seasoned professional looking for a quick refresher, this guide will unravel the mysteries of design lingo.

1. Vector Graphics:

Vector graphics are digital images created using geometric shapes like points, lines, and curves. They are resolution-independent, meaning they can be scaled up or down without loss of quality.

2. Pixel (Raster) Graphics:

Pixel graphics, or raster graphics, are made up of individual pixels arranged in a grid. Enlarging raster images can lead to loss of quality due to pixelation.

3. Typography:

Typography refers to the art and technique of arranging typefaces, fonts, and text in a visually appealing and legible manner.

4. Color Theory:

Color theory explores the principles of color mixing and how colors interact. It includes concepts like the color wheel, complementary colors, and color harmony.

5. Composition:

Composition involves arranging elements within a design to create a visually appealing and balanced arrangement. Concepts like rule of thirds and focal points are important.

6. Layer:

In design software, a layer is a separate level within a document that contains individual elements. Layers help organize and control the visual hierarchy of a design.

7. Gradient:

A gradient is a gradual transition between two or more colors. It can be applied to backgrounds, text, and objects to create depth and visual interest.

8. Mask:

A mask is a tool that allows you to hide or reveal parts of an image or object. It's often used for non-destructive editing and creating special effects.

9. Pixelation:

Pixelation occurs when a raster image is enlarged beyond its resolution, resulting in visible blocky pixels that degrade image quality.

10. Vectorization:

Vectorization is the process of converting raster images (pixels) into vector graphics (points, lines, and curves) for scalability and editing flexibility.

11. Saturation:

Saturation refers to the intensity or purity of a color. Highly saturated colors are vivid, while desaturated colors appear more muted.

12. DPI (Dots Per Inch):

DPI measures the resolution of an image or printed document. Higher DPI values result in crisper and more detailed output.

13. CMYK and RGB:

CMYK (Cyan, Magenta, Yellow, Key/Black) and RGB (Red, Green, Blue) are color models used for printing and digital displays, respectively.

14. Bezier Curve:

A Bezier curve is a mathematical representation used in vector graphics to create smooth and precise curves.

15. Masking:

Masking involves using a mask to control the transparency and visibility of an object or image, allowing for creative effects and adjustments.

16. Object Alignment:

Object alignment involves positioning elements relative to each other, ensuring they are evenly spaced or centered for a harmonious design.

17. Grid System:

A grid system is a framework of horizontal and vertical lines that help align and organize elements within a design for consistency and structure.

18. Saturation:

Saturation refers to the intensity or vividness of a color. High saturation means vibrant colors, while low saturation results in subdued colors.

19. Transparency:

Transparency refers to the level of opacity or see-through quality of an object or layer in a design.

20. Drop Shadow:

A drop shadow is a visual effect that creates the illusion of an object casting a shadow on the background, adding depth and dimension.

21. Embossing:

Embossing is a technique that raises elements off the surface, creating a 3D effect by simulating the appearance of depth and texture.

Conclusion: A Design Dictionary at Your Disposal

With this comprehensive guide, you've unlocked the doors to the world of design terminology and concepts. Armed with these definitions, you'll be better equipped to engage in design discussions, understand tutorials, and apply techniques effectively. As you traverse the design landscape, these key terms will serve as guiding stars, illuminating your path to creative mastery. Whether you're creating vector artwork, mastering typography, or delving into color theory, these definitions will empower you to navigate the complexities of design with clarity and confidence.